CRITICAL ESSAYS ON
SYLVIA TOWNSEND WARNER,
ENGLISH NOVELIST
1893-1978

CRITICAL ESSAYS ON SYLVIA TOWNSEND WARNER, ENGLISH NOVELIST 1893-1978

Edited by
Gill Davies
David Malcolm
John Simons

The Edwin Mellen Press
Lewiston•Queenston•Lampeter

Library of Congress Cataloging-in-Publication Data

Critical essays on Sylvia Townsend Warner, English novelist, 1893-1978 / edited by Gill Davies, David Malcolm, and John Simons.
    p. cm.
Includes bibliographical references and index.
ISBN 0-7734-5873-5
    1. Warner, Sylvia Townsend, 1893---Criticism and interpretation. I. Davies, Gill, 1948- II. Malcolm, David, 1952- III. Simons, John, 1955-

PR6045.A812Z63 2006
828'.91209--dc22

2006041904

hors série.

A CIP catalog record for this book is available from the British Library.

Front cover: Photograph of Sylvia Townsend Warner at her desk
© Courtesy of Susannah Pinney, the Sylvia Townsend Warner / Valentine Ackland Collection

Copyright © 2006 Gill Davies, David Malcolm, John Simons

All rights reserved. For information contact

The Edwin Mellen Press
Box 450
Lewiston, New York
USA 14092-0450

The Edwin Mellen Press
Box 67
Queenston, Ontario
CANADA L0S 1L0

The Edwin Mellen Press, Ltd.
Lampeter, Ceredigion, Wales
UNITED KINGDOM SA48 8LT

Printed in the United States of America

PR
6045
.A812
Z63
2006

CONTENTS

Preface   Maroula Joannou   i

Acknowledgements   vii

Introduction   Gill Davies, The Corners That Held Her: the Importance of Place in Sylvia Townsend Warner's Writing   1

Chapter 1   Margaretta Jolly, A Word is a Bridge: Death and Epistolary Form in the Correspondence of Sylvia Townsend Warner and David Garnett   11

Chapter 2   Frances Bingham, The Practice of the Presence of Valentine: Ackland in Warner's Work   29

Chapter 3   John Simons, On the Compositional Genetics of the *Kingdom of Elfin* together with a Note on Tortoises   45

Chapter 4   Mary Jacobs, Sylvia Townsend Warner and the Politics of the English Pastoral 1925-1934   61

Chapter 5	Emily M. Hinnov, A Counter-Reading to Conquest: "Primitivism" and Utopian Longing in Sylvia Townsend Warner's *Mr Fortune's Maggot*	83
Chapter 6	Rosemary Sykes, "This was a Lesson in History": Sylvia Townsend Warner, George Townsend Warner and the Matter of History	103
Chapter 7	Chris Hopkins, Sylvia Townsend Warner and the Historical Novel 1936-1948	117
Chapter 8	David Malcolm, *The Flint Anchor* and the Conventions of Historical Fiction	145

Index 163

PREFACE

Sylvia Townsend Warner (1893-1978) wrote much more than seven novels with a visionary dimension -- although it is upon these that recent critical attention has been most sustainedly focussed: she wrote superlative short stories, one hundred-and-forty-four of them published in *The New Yorker*, and some, like the carefully crafted, 'A Love Match', about transgressive sexuality (in this instance incest) as antidote to the stifling respectability that a character in the story dislikes no less than the author herself and longs to 'cast off, as someone tossing in fever wants to cast off a blanket'.[1] Townsend Warner was a considerable poet whose range stretched from the 'pastoral in the jog-trot English couplet' of her *Opus 7* (1931) to the revolutionary rhetoric of poems in *Left Review* and the gently lyrical love poems of *Whether a Dove or Seagull* (1934) boldly co-authored with Valentine Ackland, the authorship of each poem remaining undisclosed until the very end of the book. Sadly for the scholar and the general reader alike, many of Townsend Warner's poems and short stories are not available in modern editions and sizeable sections of the diaries, dating to highly productive periods of her life, as well as many important letters, have never been published.

Townsend Warner's writing is the antithesis of everything held dear in the metropolitan literary and social circles from which she judiciously removed herself early in the 1930s. From the depths of the English countryside, in the succession of homes she shared in Dorset and Norfolk with Ackland, her lover and partner-in-life, Townsend Warner identified the sclerotic, parsimonious and patriarchal arrangement of the British social order with rapier-like precision. Like the eponymous heroine of *Lolly Willowes* (1926) Townsend Warner was very sure of what was troubling her: 'If she were to start forgiving she needs forgive Society, the Law, the Church, the History of Europe, the Old Testament, great-aunt Salome and her prayer-book, the Bank of England, Prostitution, the Architect of Apsley Terrace, and half a dozen other props of civilisation. All she could do was to go on forgetting them.' (*LW*, p.150).

The characters in Townsend Warner's novels are expert in the vertiginous break with convention, the wildly improbable liaison, and the nonsensical or whimsical fancy, pursuing the Keatsian 'holiness of the heart's affections' - a term that this most anti-clerical of writers would certainly have resisted - with a doggedness that presages the demands for sexual autonomy and political freedom voiced in the sexual revolution of the 1960s and1970s and by the second wave of the feminists who ushered Warner's novels back into print in the Virago editions of *Lolly Willowes*, *The True Heart* and *Mr Fortune's Maggot* in 1978, the same year as her death.

The loving protectiveness of the orphaned servant maid for her mentally retarded bourgeois husband in *The True Heart* (1929), the bizarre attachment of an erstwhile London bank clerk to a haplessly, uncomprehending boy pupil on a remote south sea island in *Mr Fortune's Maggott* (1927) and the grand same-sex passion of a genteel Englishwoman for a disreputable, Jewish, itinerant, story-telling revolutionary in *Summer Will Show* (1936) exemplify Townsend Warner's impatience with the obstacles of convention, respectability, and decorum obstructing her subjects' paths to happiness.

An accomplished stylist with the brilliance, technical virtuosity and inventiveness that link her obviously to the later innovative writers, Angela Carter and Jeanette Winterson, Townsend Warner had little time for the leaden quality of much of the historical fiction of the 1930s, as Rosy Sykes points out in this collection, and little love for the modishness of much modernist experimentation of her day. As Gillian Beer puts it, 'Townsend Warner's work 'abuts the

Modernist: it uses surreal oppositions, nonsense strides, narrative fractures and shifting scales. It is nevertheless pellucid, determined and mischievous rather than allusive and indeterminate.' [2]

The emphasis on the historical and the material in this essay collection is one to which the author would have warmed. History for Townsend Warner not only opened the door to the riches of a past that could be imaginatively invoked as if it belonged to all and sundry, it also unlocked the present. Townsend Warner permits her characters no sanctuary from the materiality of existence. Even her nuns in her medieval abbey in *The Corner that Held Them* (1948) cut off from the world by marshes - Townsend Warner's synecdoche for the beleaguered Britain of the 1940s - imbibe of the 'make-do-and mend' mentality of World War Two, admonished to 'be more economical: to darn little holes before they became large ones, to be sparing of fuel', exhorted to be ever mindful of the 'high price of pins, the extravagance of little loaves, the wastage of candles' (*TCTHT*, p. 33).

Townsend Warner thought of *After the Death of Don Juan* (1938) as a work concerned with her own century; as a 'parable if you like the word, or an allegory or what you will, of the political chemistry of the Spanish War, with Don Juan – more of Moliere than of Mozart – developing as the Fascist of the Piece.'[3] The artisans' thirst for knowledge 'about the Chartists, the poor-law, the franchise, the Fenians, the amount of bacon eaten by English peasants, the experiments of the Co-operatives' (*SWS,* p. 241) in *Summer Will Show* not only brings to mind the questioning spirit of mid-nineteenth-century revolutionary France but also the yearning for education and self-improvement among the labouring men in Townsend Warner's Dorset in the 1930s. *The Flint Anchor* (1954), the last of the historical novels, and the one in which Townsend Warner appears the most concerned with delineating interior states of being, demanded revision because it was 'swaddled in old woollen rags of psychology, motives, allusions, explainings'[4] which do not always sit comfortably with a narrative set in nineteenth-century rural Norfolk.

As Mary Jacobs reminds us in her essay, the English countryside that Townsend Warner loved is not the romanticised countryside of the occasional 'week-ender'. Rather it is a landscape dotted with working figures, sometimes tipsy, a little like Bruegel's. Townsend Warner recognised English pastoral for what it often was, a 'grim and melancholy thing'.[5] Moreover, it was through Townsend Warner and Ackland's spirited efforts to improve agricultural conditions - and particularly through a series of articles by Ackland in the journal, *Left Review* later published in book form as *Country Conditions* (1936) - that the English left intelligentsia was reminded of the human misery and exploitation hidden behind the doors of the thatched cottage and the grinding hardship endured by the agricultural labourer between the wars. After the death of Ackland, Townsend Warner wrote to Arnold Rattenbury that 'This house has the accumulation of 39 years of Valentine's wide range of interests. Today I found a handhorn which says Cuckoo. We used it to vex plain-clothes policeman in the dear thirties.'[6]

Townsend Warner was a redoubtable feminist who always regarded women's rights as inseparable from other struggles for peace, democracy and freedom. Incensed by the suggestion that government directives conscripting single women into the war effort - women with husbands and children were exempt - might compel her ' to take up employment of national importance - which means they will try to put me into a laundry', she wrote in these words to her friend, Nancy Cunard (another incorrigible, rebel who like Townsend Warner supported herself financially by writing): 'The great civil war, Nancy, that will come, and must come before the world can begin to grow up, will be fought out on this terrain of man and woman, and we must storm and hold Cape Turk before we talk of social justice.'[7]

Why, then, is such a remarkable writer still neglected? It is often suggested, as David Malcolm does in this volume, that the answer lies partly in the difficulties of categorisation: Townsend Warner is protean and unorthodox.

But is this sufficient explanation? Schooled in the internal discipline of the Communist Party and the Marxism of the 1930s which admitted no distinction between theory and practice, and demanded that its leading intellectuals were visible in public as political activists, Townsend Warner, who with Ackland had served as a medical auxiliary in Republican Spain, never renounced her left-wing politics in later life and, as a consequence, was one of the many Communist intellectuals who became literary casualties of the virulent anti-Communism of the Cold War. When Arnold Rattenbury asked her why there had been no novels after *The Flint Anchor* of 1954 she replied, ' "Nothing big enough was left to say. We had fought, we had retreated, we were betrayed, and are now misrepresented. So I melted into the background as best as I could to continue sniping. You can pick odd enemies off, you know, by aiming a short story well." ' [8]

This collection is a welcome tribute to a distinguished writer of insouciant, penetrating intelligence whose importance to the recovery of English radical traditions in writing; - lesbian, feminist, socialist, visionary and utopian - is demonstrated by the work of the contributors. As Marx wrote in his *Treatise on Feuerbach* (xi), the 'philosophers have interpreted the world. The point, however', as the writings of Townsend Warner show us, 'is to change it'.

Dr Maroula Joannou
Department of English
Anglia Polytechnic University, Cambridge.

Notes

[1] 'A Love Match' (1966), in Sylvia Townsend Warner, *A Stranger With a Bag and Other Stories* (London: Chatto and Windus, 1966), pp.94-122, p.113.

[2] Gillian Beer, 'Sylvia Townsend Warner: "The Centrifugal Kick"', in Maroula Joannou (ed.), *Women Writers of the 1930s: Gender, Politics and History* (Edinburgh: the Edinburgh University Press, 1999), pp. 76-86, p.77.

[3] Letter to Nancy Cunard dated 28 August, 1945, William Maxwell (ed.), *The Letters of Sylvia Townsend Warner* (London: Chatto and Windus, 1982), p. 51, fn.

[4] Claire Harman (ed.), *The Diaries of Sylvia Townsend Warner* (London: Chatto and Windus, 1994), p.192.

[5] Quoted by Valentine Ackland in *Country Conditions*, (London: Lawrence and Wishart,1936), p.69.

[6] Unpublished letter to Arnold Rattenbury, quoted in Wendy Mulford, *This Narrow Place: Sylvia Townsend Warner and Valentine Ackland: Life, Letters and Politics, 1930-1951* (London: Pandora, 1988), p. 61.

[7] Letter to Nancy Cunard, dated 28 April 1944, in William Maxwell (ed.), *The Letters of Sylvia Townsend Warner* (London: Chatto and Windus, 1982), p.84.

[8] Quoted by Arnold Rattenbury, 'Literature, Lying and Sober Truth: Attitudes to the Work of Patrick Hamilton and Sylvia Townsend Warner', in John Lucas (ed), *Writing and Radicalism* (London: Longman: 1996), pp. 201-244, p.230.

ACKNOWLEDGEMENTS

The editors are pleased to acknowledge the skill and patience of Trish Molyneux and Debbie Chadford in preparing the camera-ready copy, and word-processing some of the text, and the support of Edge Hill College of Higher Education in providing funds to meet the incidental expenses associated with the production of this text.

INTRODUCTION
The Corners that Held Her:
The Importance of Place in Sylvia Townsend Warner's Writing
Gill Davies

Across the wide range of Warner's writing there is a recurring preoccupation with place and how place (whether geographical locations or domestic space) determines and reflects consciousness. There has been some important critical work on Warner as a feminist and as a Marxist historical novelist, and several contributors to this volume develop those aspects of her work. I see her concern for places as another important aspect of her broadly political engagement as a writer. Place is as central to the major novels as is her concern for history; it is a constant reference in her life and autobiographical writing; and it even forms the structural basis for her biography of T H White. Despite the inevitable requirements of visits to London in her developing career, Warner remained a strongly non-metropolitan, largely non-urban writer. She lived away from the city throughout her life but nevertheless avoided the stigma of being considered a 'regional' or a 'ruralist' writer. Her spatial subject matter is most frequently concerned with margins and borders, with the periphery rather than the centre (just as she is concerned with marginal or exploited social groups and individuals). Laura Willowes leaves London for Great Mop; Timothy Fortune goes from London to St Fabien then on to the even more remote island of Fanua; Sophia Willoughby leaves England for a hitherto unknown Paris, socially mixed and far away from familiar bourgeois spaces; the grandees of Seville are forced to encounter the neglected wastes of Andalucia; and a group of French nuns are shocked to find themselves in the backwater of Oby. The setting of *The Flint Anchor* is Loseby, literally on the edge of England, a place of profound provinciality, far from the metropolitan centre.

As a writer with a feminist understanding of the importance of the concrete and the everyday, Warner also used place to emphasise the importance of frequently marginalised domestic space. Her understanding of class and gender politics is rooted in the knowledge from place. She is interested in locations with a history that incorporates the lives of ordinary people and their everyday things. In fiction and non-fiction she celebrates simple and ordinary places (Dorset villages, household interiors, simple objects and domestic pleasures). Warner's account of her developing understanding of country living and its politics (for a series in *The Countryman* appropriately called 'The Way by Which I Have Come') is a detailed realisation of the history and materiality of place in people's lives, contesting the sentimental, urban middle class idealisation of country life. She dates her ceasing to be a 'townee' to the time when, rather like Lolly Willowes, she found an isolated place on an ordnance survey map and went to live there.

The collection of letters and autobiographical narrative, *I'll Stand by You*, begins with a house and continues to foreground the various houses and moves she made throughout her life with Valentine Ackland. The centrality to a relationship of houses and making a home is perhaps a particularly female perspective, but it was also bound up with the need to have somewhere to write - the importance of a good place. She emphasises the importance of living in a community, acknowledging the lives of the working people around them, and has a strong sense of the responsibilities of the 'stewardship' of a particular place. She writes of the pleasure she and Valentine take in their house and garden, their cats, and the work involved in this life. This description of 'Miss Green' (the first house they lived in together) is typical:

> And there, at the end of the journey, was the late Miss Green: her windows open, her walls milk-white, the coral-pink paint on her woodwork and Mr. Miller the carpenter at that moment putting up shelves. There was the

garden, cleaned and dug and raked smooth, and looking twice as large for it. There was old Mrs. Moxon with a bunch of flowers, waiting to tell me how well Valentine had dug and what a great heap of bindweed and couch-grass roots had been burned to wholesome ashes. And there was Valentine....[1]

In this collection, Frances Bingham's essay underlines the importance of place in the imagination of both writers. She discusses Warner's and Ackland's shared "country of the mind" and in a section full of spatial imagery argues that they had a "shared intellectual landscape" and,

certain images ... are used repeatedly by both writers - the river, the moon, the all-important landscape, gardens and growing things, animals, especially cats. Warner makes these motifs reappear in her stories with the familiarity of home.[2]

While space and place are important in the rather general senses outlined above, it is also the case that place has a function in the novels that is crucial to the realisation of Warner's vision. Her representation of place makes ideas concrete, exposes reality and its contradictions, and helps to provide a vivid sense of change and movement in society. In particular I see place informing her major fiction where it is combined with a detailed and materialist understanding of history to produce very powerful insights. Wendy Mulford says that Warner 'went beyond character and individual relationships as the motive force in her later novels, influenced by the Marxist aspiration of making "society itself, rather than the individual, the subject" ' [3] and it is partly as a result of her intense realisation of place that this de-individualising process can nevertheless not seem arid or de-humanising. Warner, perhaps in contrast to more traditional Marxist historical or realist novelists,[4] fused time and place in a way which is interestingly close to Bakhtin's theoretical model of the chronotope in fiction. Bakhtin explains it in the following way:

We will give the name *chronotope* [literally "time space"] to the intrinsic connectedness of temporal and spatial relationships that are artistically expressed in literature.... In the ... chronotope, spatial and temporal indicators are fused into one carefully thought-out, concrete whole.Time, as it were, thickens,takes on flesh, becomes artistically visible; likewise, space becomes charged and responsive to the movements of time, plot and history. This intersection of axes and fusion of indicators characterizes the artistic chronotope.[5]

What Warner is doing in her most important novels is realising this kind of social time-space. *After the Death of Don Juan,. Summer Will Show,* and *The Corner That Held Them,* in particular, provide instances of the Bakhtinian chronotope as a way of focusing on society rather than individuals. Moreover, their focus on societies undergoing significant change and crisis is realised through the representation of place almost as much as through the representation of historical time. In his discussion of the concept of the chronotope, some of Bakhtin's examples are the road, the public square, and the alien miraculous world. In Warner's novels we might identify houses and settlements as key chronotopes. Examples include Blandamer, the English country house, contrasted with the Left Bank house in Paris (in *Summer Will Show)*; the convent (in *The Corner That Held Them)*; and the tropical island in *Mr. Fortune's Maggot.*

Warner's first novel, *Lolly Willowes,* does not deploy time and space in the way that characterises her later novels. Nevertheless, it is an emerging preoccupation. The novel opens with Laura's forced move from the country to London, contrasting what she hopes London will offer - "shops, processions of the Royal Family and of the unemployed, the gold tunnel at Whiteley's, and the brilliance of the streets by night" (4) - with a more mundane and restrictive reality. Hers is a tourist's or outsider's view, because she does not belong, cannot be rooted there. Her identity is bound up with place but she does not yet know which one. The revelation of Great Mop, the village in the Chilterns where she decides to live after reading about it in a guide book, is a contrast both with Lady Place - the family home in the country - and with London. It is a historic but ordinary village where she learns how to live. In some ways, this is quite a traditional, pastoral use of place to situate the parable about Laura's independence, liberty, and self-discovery. However, as Mary Jacobs shows in this collection,[6] Warner's understanding and use of the pastoral in this period is both subtle and complex.

In *Mr. Fortune's Maggot,* Warner continues her subtly ironic use of the pastoral. Timothy Fortune, like Laura, wants to leave his old life to find himself but in changing from a London bank clerk to a missionary in the Pacific, he finds the opposite of what he anticipates. The novel satirises the idea that place itself can be transformative; he imagines signs in nature and thinks in cliches about prelapsarian islanders: "It would be a beautiful estate to live among them and gather their souls as a child gathers daisies in a field." (138) Nevertheless, it is through his extensive encounter with that place that Timothy's awakening comes about. After his loss of faith, and his decision to leave a paradise that seemingly exists outside time, he returns to a world dominated by the temporal and spatial crises of European politics and the Great War.

Summer Will Show develops Warner's materialist use of time-place. In this novel, her extraordinarily vivid and precise representation of history is frequently expressed through the realisation of place. The novel opens with an evocation of a very specific time and place: Sophia, as a child, is remembering a trip to see the Duke of Wellington. The scene described shows the English gentry glorying in their inherited wealth and power. In a brilliant shift from memory to the present, then into the future, we are shown the child's "consciousness of being an heiress, the point advancing on the future, as it were, of that magnificent triangle in which Mr. and Mrs. Aspen of Blandamer House, Dorset, England, made up the other two apices." (267) The memory is followed by an equally concrete emphasis on the present, established through place: the same view, but now 1847 and Sophia is mistress of a flourishing estate.

> Further plantations, an improved breed of cows at the home farm, the lake dredged and a walk of mown grass and willow trees carried round it, the library windows enriched with coloured glass, and a more respectable tenantry For now the Aspen triangle was reversed, and she, the hind apex,

propelled forward its front of Damian and Augusta, even as now she was propelling them towards the lime-kiln. (268)

Place of course enshrines wealth and privilege but, in addition, the recurring spatial metaphor of the triangle of inheritance is repeated, with the irony that this will not come to pass: the children will die, and Sophia will leave England and the house and all it represents. The narrative removes Sophia to places where she is not in control or respected: first, to the lime kiln, where her children contract their fatal illness, infected by the peasants their family is exploiting. And secondly, to Minna Lemuel's Left Bank house in a part of Paris Sophia has not previously visited except when being "taken to see something historical" (347). However, this is where she will undergo her <u>contemporary</u> political education. Just as chapter 1 opens with a memory of the political and cultural history of a place, so chapter 2 also begins with "the first thing I can remember": Minna's account of her Eastern European Jewish origins.

After the Death of Don Juan concerns itself with Spain and with the land, not with the picturesque landscape. Land ownership shapes the lives of the peasants and their physical environment. The novel emphasises the neglected estate, the poverty of the village and the dilapidation of the castle. The landscape itself is vividly presented as historical evidence of exploitation - not just the peasants tending olive trees that are too old and that they cannot afford to replace, but also in the character of Don Saturno, the 'liberal' landowner who plans to introduce irrigation but whose previous 'fads' are manifested in the dilapidated 'English' garden and the neglected sheep. Don Juan's proto-fascist takeover is encapsulated in the conversation with his father about the family estate of Tenorio Viejo. Don Saturno thinks his son will help with the slow process of reform, but Don Juan replies,

> "I hate the past, I hate the old. It is the new place I am interested in.... I have no intention of being a philanthropist. It is my own good that interests me abolish the rents and take over the land again" (256-7)

The last sight of the landscape the old man has, before being deposed by his son, is of the place moulded by his personal history, but into which the future is now coming, in the shape of soldiers who will defeat both the peasants and the old order. This chronotope summarises the novel's political theme:

> He looked at the landscape he had known all his life, at the place he called his. There was the river-bed, the poplar-trees, the speckled olive-yards, the green bands of the maize, the road. He saw something compact that moved at a steady pace along the road. A cloud of dust moved with it, and out of the dust flashed sharp prickles of light. (284)

In her next novel, *The Corner That Held Them*, there is even more detailed description of place used to establish 14th century England and the history of the convent over thirty years. Warner's careful research underpins the fictional details of place fused with history to create a sense of a total world. For example,

> With a manor abounding in reeds and supplied with a sufficiency of timber One might think it an easy matter to make a covered way between kitchen and refectory and some makeshift sort of cloister. But the wood was not seasoned, the reeds were not cut or were not dried, the labour was not available, the time of year was not suitable: in short, the newcomers were unwelcome.(577)

The narrative voice at first seems to be setting the scene, at an ironic distance, but it also takes on the moods and views of characters as they pass through the time and place of the novel, establishing a complex structure of feeling. Bakhtin explains this as the conjunction of time and place - 'Time, as it were, thickens, takes on flesh, becomes artistically visible'. This can be seen in the following example, typical of the way in which the novel builds a subtle sense of history from small instances. Responses to the Black Death, social hierarchy, women's lives, all emerge through the busy, idiomatic conversation in the dining hall:

> Her musing was interrupted by the sound of horses being halted outside the gate-house and a fluster of unfamiliar voices. William de Stoke, whose daughter was a novice in the house, had sent to fetch the girl away, having

> heard that the pestilence was already at Oby. He had sent a large retinue of servants, and all of them were hungry and required feeding.
> While the de Stoke people ate they talked. Though there had been pestilences often enough there had never been, they said, such a pestilence as this. It travelled faster than a horse, it swooped like a falcon, and those whom it seized on were so suddenly corrupted that the victims, still alive and howling in anguish, stank like the dead. ...All across Europe it had come, and now it would traverse England, and nothing could stop it, wherever there were men living it would seek them out, and turn back, as a wolf does, to snap at the man it had passed by. (582)

This is the opposite of the 'heritage' reconstruction of history in much popular fiction and film. And it is not simply a result of research, and fidelity to 'the facts', but specifically a combination of those elements with a concrete <u>placing</u> of voice and period detail. Warner's final novel, *The Flint Anchor*, shows no lessening of the author's concern to link place and time in complex and substantial ways. Historical dates are carefully noted, events and their impact on this peripheral place recorded, the shifting customs and fashions and the physical appearance of things lovingly detailed, and the interaction of the human characters with this chronotope delicately and subtly delineated. Houses, streets, local mores, historical and personal events are interwoven here, too, at the end of Warner's novelistic career, as they were at its height.

Taken together, the essays in this volume testify to the extraordinary range and diversity of Warner's writing. They cover her letters, poetry, novels and short stories. There are nevertheless, some common themes. Several writers insist on the importance of the writer's life and experience (in the context of a particular history). Margaretta Jolly[7] discusses the correspondence between Warner and David Garnett, demonstrating the importance of reading letters and autobiography with careful critical and theoretical attention. The breaking down of barriers between the literary and the autobiographical is also part of Frances Bingham's project in her essay. And Rosemary Sykes[8] argues for the importance of the influence of Warner's early formation under the tutelage of her historian father.

Different aspects of Warner's engagement with history are addressed in several of the essays in this collection. Simons, like Bingham, is interested in Warner's sources and her use of myth, fairy tales and folk tales. His essay demonstrates the extraordinary richness of reference and scholarship in the late stories, *Kingdoms of Elfin*[9]. Sykes examines Warner's study of history, emphasising her understanding of its materials, noting that like fiction it has to be shaped and constructed. Chris Hopkins[10] discusses the changing form of the historical novel in *Summer Will Show*, *After the Death of Don Juan* and *The Corner that Held Them*, relating the changes to Warner's involvement in contemporary debates about history and its narrative representation. David Malcolm[11] looks at the tension between the historical and a-historical elements in Warner's fiction, concentrating on her last novel, *The Flint Anchor* (1954). Emily Hinnov[12] analyses Warner's critique of colonialist values and her radical re-working of modernist appropriations of 'primitivism' in *Mr. Fortune's Maggot*. The aim of all the essays in this collection is to stimulate interest in the work of Sylvia Townsend Warner and to confirm her reputation as an important and original twentieth century writer.

Edge Hill College of Higher Education, Lancashire

Works Cited

Warner, Sylvia Townsend. *Lolly Willowes* 1926

_____. *Mr. Fortune's Maggot* 1927

_____. *Summer Will Show* 1931

_____. *The Corner That Held Them* 1948 all reprinted in *Four in Hand: A Quartet of Novels*. Introduction by William Maxwell. New York: W.W. Norton & Co.,1986

_____. *After the Death of Don Juan* 1938. London: Virago, 2002

_____. *T.H. White A Biography* 1967; Oxford: Oxford University Press, 1989

_____. *I'll Stand By You: Selected Letters of Sylvia Townsend Warner and Valentine Ackland with Narrative by Sylvia Townsend Warner*. Ed. Susan

Pinney. London: Pimlico,1998

_____. 'The Way By Which I Have Come', *The Countryman* vol.xlx (July 1939) pp. 472-486

Notes
[1] *I'll Stand By You* p.11

[2] Frances Bingham, 'The Practice of the Presence of Valentine', below pp.29-44

[3] Introduction to *After the Death of Don Juan*, p.x

[4] Chris Hopkins has a very interesting discussion of this in his essay 'Sylvia Townsend Warner and the Marxist Historical Novel', *Literature and History* 3rd series vol.4 no. 1 Spring 1995

[5] M.M. Bakhtin, 'Forms of Time and of the Chronotope in the Novel', *The Dialogic Imagination* ed. Michael Holquist; tr. Caryl Emerson & Michael Holquist, Austin: Univ. of Texas Press 1981 p.84

[6] Mary Jacobs, 'Sylvia Townsend Warner and the Politics of the English Pastoral 1925-1934' below pp.61-82

[7] Margaretta Jolly, 'A Word is a Bridge: Death and Epistolary Form in the Correspondence of Sylvia Townsend Warner and David Garnett', below pp.11-28

[8] Rosemary Sykes, '"This was a lesson in history": Sylvia Townsend Warner, George Townsend Warner and the matter of History' below pp.103-116

[9] John Simons, 'On the Compositional Genetics of the Kingdom of Elfin together with a Note on Tortoises', below pp.45-60

[10] Chris Hopkins, 'Sylvia Townsend Warner and the Historical Novel 1936-1948' below pp.117-144

[11] David Malcolm, '*The Flint Anchor* and the Conventions of Historical Fiction' below pp.145-162

[12] Emily Hinnov, 'A Counter Reading to Conquest: "Primitivism" and Utopian longing in Sylvia Townsend Warner's *Mr Fortune's Maggot*' below pp.83-102

CHAPTER 1

A Word is a Bridge:
Death and Epistolary Form in the Correspondence of Sylvia Townsend Warner and David Garnett

Margaretta Jolly

'A correspondence', Sylvia Townsend Warner once reflected, 'kept up over a length of years with never a meeting is a bridge which with every letter seems more elastically reliable, but it is a bridge that only carries the weight of one person at a time. When the correspondents meet it collapses', she brutally continued, 'and they have to founder their way to the footing of actuality' (Warner, *T.H. White: A Biography* 219). Letters are indeed an 'elastic bridge', as magical as they are apparently reliable in the capacity to stretch across any distance or time. Yet Warner reminds us of the fragility at the heart of this protean form. Far from the solid and inflexible ground of 'actuality', an epistolary relationship is created out of the mutual projections of two writers, which, in another of Warner's formulations, always risk being 'slightly out of focus' (143).

In the following discussion, I build on Warner's image to explore the fictions of letter-writing as a positive aspect of the form not just for the correspondents themselves but for the reader of published letters. The ambiguity and intermittency of their appeal to the other can produce powerful literary effects. But we should avoid trying to fit letters into the classical literary mould of a unity constructed by a single author. Too often critics find themselves overemphasising the monologue at the expense of the dialogue in trying to recoup a correspondence's formal complexity. In my view, it is the tension between monologue and dialogue, fracture and unity, which creates letters' literary interest, drawing on the 'sumptuous, desirable, yet anxiety-ridden interlude' of the epistolary experience itself (Hallett 111). Warner's own exquisite fifty-six year correspondence with the writer David Garnett exemplifies these tensions. Jovial and harmonious in style and sensibility, the underlying delicacy of its architecture emerges through the editorial intervention of Garnett's son, Richard Garnett. The double-edged nature of epistolary art is most obvious in Warner and Garnett's dryly aesthetic discussion of mortality followed by the literal interruption of their correspondence with Warner's death. In conclusion, I return to Warner's image of a bridge that 'carries the weight of only one person at a time', as a salutory reminder of the irony – and poetry – of epistolary reassurance.

The peculiar art of correspondence

The last thirty years have seen a small but persistent effort within literary criticism to theorise real letters with some of the rigour now given to other auto/biographical genres. These efforts are characterised by an interest in the constructions that lie within or against the apparent identity of the letter as communication. Praising 18th century epistolarians like Swift and Johnson, Bruce Redford exemplifies the humanist critic's method of discovering more 'art' in letters than is generally supposed:

> Epistolary discourse fashions a distinctive world at once internally consistent, vital and self-supporting. The letters of a master thereby escape from their origins as reservoirs of fact: coherence replaces correspondence as the primary standard of judgement. (Redford 9)

Redford's criteria of 'coherence' tests assumptions that letters are merely chaotic and occasional, showing what can lift communications out of the minutely specific contexts of private relationship. But in doing so, he restricts his aesthetic criteria to the traditional ones of transcendence over time and place through unified form and authorial autonomy. Valuing 'coherence over correspondence' too drastically represses the relationship that by definition sustains correspondence, even if it allows a refreshing escape from 'fact'. Redford's formulation also typifies the tendency to reinstate the individual 'master' as the focus of creativity (his focus on 'letters' rather than 'correspondence' is symptomatic). For the public reader as well as the original addressee, it is as much the vicissitudes and open-endedness of time, place and relationship in epistolary plots that fascinate.

This abstraction from the correspondents' relationship is ironically repeated in structuralist and deconstructive approaches to letters, of which a turning point was the French critic Bernard Bray's reading of Madame de Sévigné's letters to her daughter. Challenging inherited views of her thousand-plus letters as outpourings of a perhaps obsessive love, he claimed they were determined by an elaborate 'système épistolaire', more stylistically than psychologically motivated (Horowitz 17). This system comprised the material conditions of the postal system, the social functions of letter-writing in transferring information from the court to the provinces, and the aristocracy's interest in the analysis of the passions. Bray's move usefully reinserted social and linguistic structure in a form so heavily determined since the seventeenth century as both spontaneous and private. But the letter more accurately illustrates the general paradox that any exchange is at once coded and idiosyncratic; synchronic and diachronic. If the impulse to address another cannot be recuperated under any straightforward heading of individual intention or creativity, neither can it simply be reduced to the same terms as the code itself. Louise Horowitz took up this point in arguing that although Bray was correct to analyse the letters as texts, he went too far in voiding them of any real affective content, consequently overemphasising Sévigné's conventionality and public literary ambition (25). Horowitz, instead, sees the letters' literary pull as the result of Sévigné's working out of a personal fantasy of her daughter as a 'princesse lointaine', through the consolation of writing:

> Time, space, description, the entire relationship with Mme de Grignan appear to have their own textually limiting status, to have acquired a striking independence from their affective origin... this altering process... is what ultimately accounts for the wide public appreciation of the letters over the centuries. (23)

Horowitz says that the double movement of a narcissistic pleasure in both desire and writing 'may be the most genuine mark of letter-writing'. But if Horowitz preserves the story of a specific relationship as part of what may interest a public reader, acknowledging the complex psychology of letter-writing itself, she still focuses on only one side of the correspondence. A more generous formulation is Alvaro Ribeiro's work on Samuel Johnson's letters to Hester Thrale. Ribeiro also avoids falsely opposing communication and expression by locating the aestheticising process in the impulse to communicate. But he postulates that it is the 'insistent, creative reaching out from the time- and place-bound self to the other in the converse of the pen that suggests to me a possible theoretical framework for understanding the genre' (Ribeiro 104, my emphasis). For Ribeiro, features such as the classic 'five point' rhetorical structure of a letter, which elegantly enshrines its 'real business' in the middle of formalised salutations and closures, are aspects of communion that reveal the letter to be a form of gift. Perhaps we should think of this as the ideal, in the sense Virginia Woolf defined letter-writing as 'the humane art which owes its origin to the love of friends' (Woolf).

The letter's *mutual*, if not always equal, creation of meaning by reader and writer naturally pushes us beyond theories that inscribe either party's absolute determinacy, in part simply because they exchange position. Jacques Derrida for this reason used the letter as the quintessential form for showing the errancy of meaning (Derrida). But the letter equally metonymises meaning's endless arrival. Philosophies of language that begin from the premise of dialogue rather than deferral are far better able to encompass both the narcissistic and gift-giving elements of letter-writing, and indeed, it is in one of the founding texts of 'dialogic' literary theory, Valentin Volosinov's 1929 'Marxism and the Philosophy of Language', that we find the bridge that so interested Warner, occur as a metaphor for language itself:

> Word is a two-sided act. As word, it is precisely the product of the reciprocal relationship between speaker and listener, addresser and addressee. Each and every word expresses the 'one' in relation to the 'other'. I give myself verbal shape from another's point of view, ultimately, from the point of view of the community to which I belong. A word is a bridge thrown between myself and another. If one end of the bridge depends on me, then the other depends on my addressee. (Voloshinov 58, his emphasis).

Dialogic theory of this kind restores more than a historical context to semiotics in its optimistic premise that signifier and signified, subject and object, self and other, are perpetually related rather than alienated, as post-structuralist theory commonly has it (Pearce 10). Dialogic approaches uncover dialogue within monologic genres like the novel and in techniques like free indirect speech and the 'heteroglossia' of mixed dialects. But if to some extent all monologue is ultimately an abstraction (Holquist 59), letters make plain that relationships are no more equal than they are easy. Warner's image of the turnstile bridge, ironically concealing monologue within dialogue, reminds us that every utterance is 'a border phenomenon ... drenched in social factors' (61).

Dialogue, in the expanded form that dialogic theory conceives of it, includes the politics of the unsaid, the intonation of negotiation. Nowhere is this more painfully evident than in Warner's own extensive correspondence with her troubled partner Valentine Ackland, with whom she lived for 39 years (Warner,

Ackland and Pinney). Warner and Ackland did not go a day without writing when they were apart, and sometimes even when they were together, most heart wrenchingly when Warner had agreed to abscond herself in a hotel so Valentine could pursue her affair with Elizabeth Wade White. The luxuriously inventive protestations of undying love and dependence on both sides were as much compensation for the tragedy that Valentine brought to their relationship, and their negotiation with the wider world as a lesbian couple, as they were the unstoppable demonstration of their intimacy (Castle, "The Will to Whimsy"). Mismatched in their games, with Ackland always jealous of Warner's literary superiority and Warner watching Ackland's sexual talents turning their aim elsewhere, Warner competed with epistolary gifts that Ackland in the end could not live without. Warner's editorial narrative does not quite admit to this, wanting still to present the letters as commemoration of a triumphant life-long passion. Yet the very turn-taking of their voices conveys the uncertainty of love, a bridge being written by those who were almost always physically together.

Although the tragic-comic beauty of Warner and Ackland's correspondence would provide an eloquent occasion for acknowledging the relationships involved in all writing, I take Warner's much happier correspondence with David Garnett as my example precisely because it was much more simply literary. As is the way with marriages and friendships, Garnett was more similar to Warner in his fundamentally comic temperament than her beloved but depressive Valentine. In addition, the fact that it was assembled by Garnett's son rather than either correspondent, shows a further level of contingency – a further level of relationship. The editor's contribution as mediator with the public reader is another, also neglected, element of an aesthetics of letter-writing. Narrative, as much as narcissism or empathy, structures what we read as epistolary selves, including such pragmatic concerns as having a full sequence and both sides of a correspondence. In other words, the aesthetic unity of coherence, and, with it, our vision of incoherence and loss, is partly imported. The rest of this paper explores Warner and Garnett's own correspondence as a tribute not just to the relationships at the heart of letter-writing, but of letter-editing and reading as well.

One-person bridges and mortal love

Professional authors who write a lot of letters luxuriate in what William Maxwell, editor of Warner's *Selected Letters*, describes as 'throwing away one of their better efforts' (Warner, *Selected Letters* viii). Elizabeth Bishop, a consummate letter-writer, called it 'writing off-duty' (Paulin).[1] Warner was such a writer. Much like her short stories, her unfailingly elegant letters abound with matchless wit (Castle, *The Apparitional Lesbian: Female Homosexuality and Modern Culture* 74). She often wrote several a day, and, very unusually, rarely repeated herself in any of them; her regular correspondents treasured the thousands that she wrote. Although Warner did intend for many to be published (she even wrote a connecting narrative for her correspondence with Valentine), Claire Harman observes that her most highly valued friendships were founded and maintained by transatlantic correspondences, contending that she 'loved, and needed, the uncluttered intellectual intimacy which depended on distance and separateness and which such correspondence allowed' (Harman 309).

Warner's relationship with David Garnett was one patterned on this 'uncluttered intellectual intimacy'. Their correspondence, which began when she was 29 and he 30, lasted until just a month before she died, age 85. Published in 1994, it amply demonstrates the qualities of coherence considered characteristic of great writing. But just as essential is its literary gift-giving and subtle politics. The letters sprang from the mutual literary interest of two professional writers in the early stages of both their careers, both writing in a style oblique to their high modernist contemporaries. In 1920, Warner was working as a musicologist and writing the odd poem. Garnett, of a more literary background, was a publisher's reader and partner of the Soho bookshop of Birrell and Garnett. Stephen Tomlin introduced them; they walked over the desolate Essex marshes in an epiphanic moment of communion (Warner, *Selected Letters* xiii). Garnett gave her the notebook in which she began keeping her first diary (Castle, "The Will to Whimsy" 237), and more importantly, prompted Chatto and Windus to publish Warner's first collection of poetry, *The Espalier* (1925). Lolly Willowes, the novel with which she made her name, came out a few months later. Forever after, she saw him as having launched her literary career, writing in 1966:

> If it had not been for you, by now I would probably have given up writing poems and keeping them in a drawer. And if I had written any prose it would have appeared in the Musical Times. (Garnett 97)

Garnett replied:

> You should not write such letters. You make me insufferably proud, and it will require the united efforts of Angelica [his wife] and my three daughters batting me over the head with a spoon and exclaiming 'Down, wanton, down!' - as though I were an eel in the pan - to reduce me to my proper place. Nobody has ever had such a wonderful letter. (97)

Garnett did not see Warner as a mentor in the same way, but he was equally eager for her responses to each of his publications, the occasion that usually prompted each of them to write for the first decades of their correspondence. The tone is set by this mutual admiration and encouragement and although it modulates to a more serious key, the echo of gratified ambition remains. Both writers were extraordinarily prolific and able to live off their writing throughout their lives.

This narrowly literary focus dominates the correspondence until both were in their 70s, only a third of the way through the collection. This is in part due to a twenty-three year hiatus in their correspondence, which Richard Garnett suggests was a result of Valentine Ackland's jealousy of Garnett. (Maxwell concurs with this. Warner, *Selected Letters* 247) When it is resumed, however, there is little sense of the passing of this time. The settings are the same: Warner had been installed in Maiden Newton, Dorset, since 1937, he at Hilton Hall, in Huntingdonshire since 1924. The writerly games are also familiar: they are as ferociously productive as ever. They make no reference to the events of those twenty-three years, during which Warner fell in love and settled down with Ackland, left heterosexual forays behind, worked for the British Communist Party and went to Spain to support the Spanish Civil War; during which Garnett was Literary Editor for *The New Statesman and Nation*, worked for the Air Ministry during the war, lost his first wife Ray Marshall to breast cancer and married Angelica Bell, the young daughter of Vanessa Bell, fathering four daughters by her in addition to his two sons by Ray.

It is a literary project that rejuvenates their correspondence, but one that also spotlights its own status as a creative form. In 1964, at the age of 70, Warner was asked to write the biography of T.H. White, an idiosyncratic author best known for his rewrite of Malory's Arthurian epic, *The Once and Future King*, and a close friend of David Garnett. After giving Garnett first refusal, she accepted, while he eventually decided to edit his own correspondence with White. Both are trying to write about White, a subject in which their own status as friends and readers is implicated, and it forces them to be explicit about the different kinds of truths that letters and biographies can tell. Garnett advises Warner that:

> The chief thing in a biography - not that I know anything about writing them - is to exhibit your subject, or let him exhibit himself, from all angles, which is what a tailor does when making one a suit.
> Luckily for you, White exhibited himself in the most contradictory ones. In fact his metier was to do so. He was inspired by his own multiform image, which is not how you and I work. (74)

There were limits to the 'angles' that Warner could show White from, as she discovered his diary accounts of sadistic and paedophiliac desires. Jan Montefiore has shown how Warner eventually found a way to 'be honest' in concentrating on his identity as a writer rather than his sexuality (Montefiore). But this solution still left Warner struggling with the form:

> Dearest David,... White is killing me. I don't see how I can give the book any air of proportion. Do you realise that all his creative work was over by 1945? From then on, he splutters and gutters. If I could use his lust and rage and frenzy and defeat over the – boy I could make a real dragon's tail ending. But everybody's bloody feelings are in the way, and if I observe them I shall be reduced to the portrait of a frustrated Scout Master. (83)

Both of them feel as strongly about aesthetic balance as free speech. Garnett argues that biography can bring the two together since truth is more interesting when it is not sanitised. But Warner amuses him on the limit-case of White:

> I won't cheat; and have a beginning idea of what I can't do, which is a bottomless pit. It is a sad reflection, darling David, that after all the years intelligent people like ourselves have been illuminating English society it is still totally impossible to be honest... (73)

Garnett considered that Warner was successful in her enterprise, confessing with wonder that she seemed to know his friend better than he did himself. He dedicated his eventual edition of the *White/Garnett* letters in 1968 to her with the words: 'To Sylvia Townsend Warner, who in her biography of T.H. White has given us the real man' (White and Garnett). But this was after some revealing doubts about the very different - indeed, 'false' - version of White he felt emerged from his letters:

> I wish you here, because I wanted to tell you, to confess to you, by word of mouth what I hesitate to say on paper. The fact is I am horribly bored,

> not by Tim himself, but my friendship with him exemplified in all those idiotic solemn letters written from false premises. (Garnett 94)

Warner tried to reassure him without further dishonesty:

> As for the D.G./T.H.W letters, why shouldn't they wait? If you leave them long enough, they will come back to life, and you will be able to accept the false premises as part of the set-up: which they are. True, I don't at the moment see how you can editorially remark: At this moment I hated his guts. But you will find a way, if you leave them to simmer at the back of the stove. (95)

It is these same 'false premises' that Warner described in the more subtle terms of the 'bridge that only carries the weight of one person at a time'. As she tells it in the biography, however, her formal observation of a covert monologue is immediately and comically returned to the story of Garnett and White's very real relationship:

> When White reached Hilton Hall on the evening of September 25th he and Garnett met with affection; for six years the bridge had carried a traffic of sympathy, advice, enlivening nonsense, exasperations, understanding and misunderstanding, dependence and assurance. It could have been the happy reunion they had earned by remaining alive to each other if the dogs had not added their overwhelming goodwill. Garnett was irked by 'the noise and physical presence of Quince, who stood four foot six on his pads and knocked everything off any table with his amiable tail and Killie, bouncing, ingratiating and all too female'. White sensed this, fled into the defensive, ... decided that Garnett knew nothing about dogs and trailed his petticoat about the war. Worse was to come. (Warner, *T.H. White: A Biography* 220)

The particular deceptions involved in Garnett's friendship with White, she suggests, were magnified by those inherent in letter-writing, indeed, the abstraction of writing itself, so graphically punctured with the image of the two noisy, bouncing dogs. Although the 'enlivening nonsense' that fills many letters seems to make them a realist genre, in fact, their reference is entirely relational. In this sense, Warner's approach is dialogical most especially in its teasing out of monologue, for it is the relationship, not any absolute truth that counts.

Warner's view of the White/Garnett letters points up the slipperiness of her own 'set-up' with Garnett, although of this, she writes nothing. Frequently declaring their mutual fondness and solidarity as the years pass, Warner and Garnett reach their eighties with the White biography having been declared a masterpiece and Garnett in full swing of a seemingly endless flow of novels. Even so, there is a complex tension between writerly affection and distance in person that makes this last and longest stage of correspondence a powerful example of the 'one-person bridge.' For example, the sharp anatomising of male sexual hypocrisy, so important to Warner's fiction, is never discussed with the womanising Garnett. This is in part due to mutual discretion about their personal relationships, but also their shared dedication to art. Precisely because of their insistent optimism over meaning's arrival, the glimpses of its errancy are poignant. From 1968 to Warner's deaths in 1978 and Garnett's in 1981, both suffered painful and tragic losses. Angelica left Garnett in 1967, Valentine died in 1969, Garnett's eldest daughter committed suicide in 1973 and an old mutual friend did so the following year. Both ended by living for years alone. For each other, they chart these events briefly and stoically: Sylvia observed that Garnett's offhand announcement on the back of an envelope that his wife has left him was 'one of the best placed sentences you have ever written' (130). Warner was meanwhile grateful for Garnett's refusal to coddle after Ackland's death:

> 8 December 1969
>
> Dear Sylvia, I send you my love.
> I love the visible world so much that it consoles me to know that it is going on: however much we mess it up - day and night, high tide and low tide, summer and winter: forever - and that we don't.

But such reflections are no help for pain and loneliness: for that there's no cure, my dear.
Well, all my love
David

2 September 1970

Dearest David, …How old we both are, my dear. Alike in that, if in nothing else. In a way, I am more like the Sylvia you first knew, for I have reverted to solitude. I live in a house too large for me, with three cats; and when the telephone rings and it is a wrong number I feel a rush of thankfulness. I was grateful to you for your letter after Valentine's death, for you were the sole person who said that for pain and loneliness there is no cure. I suppose people have not the moral stamina to contemplate the idea of no cure; and to ease their uneasiness they trot out the most astonishing placebos. I was assured I would find consolation in writing, in gardening, in religion, in tortoises, in keeping bees, in social service (the world is so full of misery); and many of these consolers were people whom I had previously found quite rational. Your only runner-up was Reynolds Stone's wife, who said, whiskey.

But when one has had one's head cut off -

Please, if only for my peace of mind, outlive Michael Holroyd. For my pleasure too, come to that.

There you are with your enormous hearth, your refrigerator, £1000 p.a., the days drawing in: you are ideally circumstanced to write to me from time to time.
With my mortal love
Sylvia (156-7)

The dogged humour and appeals to the indifferent beauty of nature grow more insistent as friends drop away, or turn to self-pity and religious comfort. Injustice, foolishness and irrationality become spectres exorcised by their superior, always amused, worldliness. Such reason and self-sufficiency is exaggerated by the pastoral setting, for both writers chose a life and retirement of relative isolation in the country. The letters abound with descriptions of gardening, harvesting, cooking, animal husbandry, recipes and passionate weather reports. Garnett keeps bees. Sylvia grows white currants. These themes of the good life, occasionally punctuated by a sardonic reference to contemporary political events, provide the classical themes of comic renewal:

14 December 1968

Self-pity is despised - but let me please give way - and despise me to your heart's content. My young birds are all fledged: I have seen them fly out of the nest. All duty is over. Yes *duty*. But what has that got to do with it? One can't stop loving as the barn owls do in October - or as the cats feel towards their mature kittens. ... Well, Sylvia, my trouble - and I think yours - is that we love life. How extraordinarily happy they must be who hate it! What a good wicket they are on! In ten years' time - universal nuclear destruction of the populations, animal and vegetable, of the earth. So in the season of Peace on Earth, I wish you a Very Merry Christmas and Glorious New Year. (149)

2 July 1973

Yes, [David] you *are* like Peacock, my dear: like Peacock in having lived on into an age of uncongenial Faith. I suppose people have to be believers. The object varies, but the devotees are much the same. I sit appalled at the sheepishness and credulity of the present iconophiles, who believe that every irregularity of mind, such as genius, can be ironed out by People who know Better, psychoanalysts, sociologists, psychotherapists, qualified social workers.
All faiths are worldly. Do you agree? - means for getting on, rising in the world, social insurance. (178)

But the virtual youth sustained by such literary sensuality is a performance that sometimes sounds shrill, particularly in Garnett's lengthy descriptions of his physical prowess. Aged 82, he recounts driving from Britain to Spain to swim in the Canaries (190-91); aged 84, finishing a 100,000-word novel, giving a huge birthday party, house-training a wild cat, and industrial-scale washing. Compare this to a diary account of Warner's of 1959, when he was 67:

> He has grown a little deaf, and at first it was uneasy, dimmed; then he began to talk about the wall-paintings discovered in Sparrow's Farm, and the pheasants made by the Women's Institute falling dead to the Victorian sportsmen... alas! he is very hurt and smouldering about Chatto and Windus's rejection of his book. (Warner and Harman 62)

To him, she wrote a week later, 'Darling David, Thank you for giving me *A Shot in the Dark*, thank you for writing it. It is an enamoured book, Stendhal could not have written of Italy more loverly.... I think Chatto and Windus were fools to turn it down' (Garnett 63). To Valentine, Warner saw David as bearing a 'mixture of shyness and a great deal of sexual condescension' (Warner, Ackland and Pinney 319), and in a letter to Bea Howe in 1975, she noted:

> David came last week, and I gave him brandy with his coffee, and some admirable fillet steak. I watched his start of delighted surprise when he sank his teeth into the first mouthful.
> After the first mutual shock of seeing ourselves so much changed for the worst, we found we had not changed so much after all, and it was a happy visit. (Warner, *Selected Letters* 203)

Her next letter to David comes out as, 'It was a pleasing astonishment to find out how well you still knew me' (Garnett 205).

Self-sufficiency as a model of aesthetic value is thus alone insufficient to explain what moves us about this correspondence, ironically because of its very centrality as both writers' personal and aesthetic ideal. Although there is nothing of the degree of hidden monologue in Garnett's correspondence with White, or the complex substitution of Warner's correspondence with Ackland, its value is measured by the costs as well as pleasures of standing alone. As with writers like Johnson and Sévigné, physical distance is transmuted into aesthetic confidence, in which a fantasy of reason and wit seems to thrive against emotion, disability and death. But even in this most coherent of correspondences, it is the contradiction between unity and disunity, teased out by editorial connection and commentary, which is so fundamental to its literary effect. The theme of transcendence is embodied in an ephemeral form that, strung together, marks the implacable march of time. The ending, which they of course, did not write, delivers this message most definitively, with the abrupt, abashed entrance of editor on stage. Sylvia died, then David did: dialogue hangs in ungainly monologue, waiting for an answer to which there is no longer any point. Contrast this to Warner's gleeful description to Garnett of a more controlled aesthetic death:

> Today I ... took out Housman's *Last Poems*.... And on the last page was THE END. As you might expect. But I suddenly had a vivid sense of the goblin pleasure A.E.H. must have had as he wrote those words, in a neat scholar's handwriting, licking dry lips, slamming that noiseless door. (206)

Epistolary bridges are always shaky in the uncertainty of the future they must be thrown towards, even when each correspondent takes such pleasure in watching the other cross over. This is not because virtual relationships are less serious or real than physical ones. On the contrary, writing's defence against the transience of the body is as simple in letters as the acknowledgement of underlying absence. Warner and Garnett's defiant dialogue shows, however, that this is a more poetic wager when it recognises that though we are not autonomous, we can also only cross the bridge alone.

Works cited

Castle, Terry. *The Apparitional Lesbian: Female Homosexuality and Modern Culture*. New York: Columbia UP, 1993.

_____. "The Will to Whimsy." *Boss Ladies, Watch Out!: Essays on Women, Sex, and Writing*. New York: Routledge, 2002. 237-44.

Derrida, Jacques. *The Post-Card: From Socrates to Freud and Beyond.* Trans. Alan Bass. Chicago: U of Chicago P, 1980.

Garnett, Richard, ed. *Sylvia and David: The Townsend Warner/Garnett Letters.* London: Sinclair-Stevenson, 1994.

Hallett, Nicky. "'Anxiously Yours': The Epistolary Self and the Culture of Concern." *Journal of European Studies* 32.2 & 3 (2002): 107-20.

Harman, Claire. *Sylvia Townsend Warner: A Biography.* London: Chatto & Windus, 1989.

Holquist, Michael. *Dialogism: Bakhtin and His World.* 2nd ed. London ; New York: Routledge, 2002.

Horowitz, Louise K. "The Correspondence of Madame De Sévigné: Letters or Belles-Lettres?" *French Forum* 6 (1981): 13-27.

Montefiore, Jan. "Sylvia Townsend Warner: Authority and the Biographer's Moral Sense." *Imitating Art: Essays in Biography.* Ed. David Ellis. London: Pluto, 1993. 124--48.

Paulin, Tom. "Newness and Nowness: The Extraordinary Brilliance of Elizabeth Bishop's Letters." *Times Literary Supplement* 29 April 1994: 3-6.

Pearce, Lynne. *Reading Dialogics.* London: Arnold, 1994.

Redford, Bruce. *The Converse of the Pen: Acts of Intimacy in the Eighteenth-Century Familiar Letter.* Chicago: U of Chicago P, 1986.

Ribeiro, Alvaro, S.J. "Real Business, Elegant Civility and Rhetorical Structure in Two Letters by Charles Burney." *Sent as a Gift: Eight Correspondents from the Eighteenth Century.* Ed. Alan T. Mckenzie. Athens, Ga: U of Georgia P, 1993. 90-108.

Voloshinov, Valentin Nikolaevich. "Marxism and the Philosophy of Language." *The Bakhtin Reader: Selected Writings of Bakhtin, Medvedev, Voloshinov.* Ed. Pam Morris. 1929 ed. London: Arnold, 1994. 50-61.

Warner, Sylvia Townsend. *Selected Letters.* Ed. William Maxwell. London: Viking Penguin, 1982.

———. *T.H. White: A Biography*. Oxford: Oxford University Press, 1989.

Warner, Sylvia Townsend, Valentine Ackland, and Susanna Pinney. *I'll Stand by You: Selected Letters of Sylvia Townsend Warner and Valentine Ackland : With Narrative by Sylvia Townsend Warner*. Pimlico ; 303. London: Pimlico, 1998.

Warner, Sylvia Townsend, and Claire Harman. *The Diaries of Sylvia Townsend Warner*. London: Chatto & Windus, 1994.

Warner, Sylvia Townsend, William Maxwell, and Michael Steinman. *The Element of Lavishness: Letters of Sylvia Townsend Warner and William Maxwell, 1938-1978*. 1st ed. Washington, D.C.: Counterpoint, 2001.

White, T. H., and David Garnett. *The White/Garnett Letters*. New York,: Viking Press, 1968.

Woolf, Virginia. "The Humane Art." *New Statesman and Nation* 8 June 1940: 726.

Notes
[1] This selection represents all of her main correspondents, except Valentine Ackland, including the novelist Bea Howe, Warner's editors at Chatto and Windus, Charles Prentice and Harold Raymond, the artistic Powys family; her cousin Oliver Warner; Jean Starr Untermeyer the American poet and translator; Julius and Queenie Lipton from the Communist Party; Nancy Cunard, the left wing writer, and Paul Nordoff, the composer. Warner's correspondence with Maxwell, who was her editor at the *New Yorker*, has been presented in more detail (See Warner, Maxwell and Steinman), as has her correspondence with Ackland (Warner, Ackland, Pinney).

CHAPTER 2

The Practice of the Presence of Valentine:
Ackland in Warner's Work

Frances Bingham

'The practice of the presence of Valentine' was the description Sylvia Townsend Warner gave to the visitations of Valentine Ackland, in dreams or visions, which she experienced after Ackland's death. (She was paraphrasing the title of one of Ackland's devotional books, in which the presence invoked is God, rather than Valentine.[1]) Just as these moments of contact were welcomed by Warner in her life, they were also incorporated into her work. I have borrowed the quotation to describe the frequent presence of Ackland in Warner's writing, whether as the recipient of coded messages, a character, an inspirational muse or simply a recurring theme or motif.

It was Warner's pleasure, and need, to include Ackland in her work in these various ways, and she must have been aware that this private practice would become increasingly publicly known. As more and more of Warner and Ackland's non-fiction is researched and published, the codes are provided with which to read these hidden messages – which were undoubtedly intended for us, Warner's future readers, to understand. She expected that her diaries and letters, and also Valentine's autobiographical writings, would be published after their deaths, and the clues which she left in them are very clear. (However, Warner's surreally cut-and-paste attitude to the use of autobiographical material frustrates any misguided attempt to draw too close comparisons between life and art.)

Recognition of the freight of private meaning which these components of Warner's work carry doesn't, obviously, explain away or belittle her powers of imbuing characters and their surroundings with enormous significance, but rather enables the reader to appreciate yet another facet of Warner's art. The hitherto often unacknowledged presence of Valentine, once recognised, gains the reader an important insight into Warner's writing, and an understanding of how she put her most profound obsession to creative use. An encyclopaedic knowledge of all Ackland and Warner's non-fictional writings, published and unpublished, is not necessary in order to apprehend the presence of Valentine. Readers of Warner's diary, the Warner/Ackland letters, and Ackland's published memoir *For Sylvia*[2], are well-equipped to recognise Valentine wherever she appears. (And, like the apparitional lesbian, she is everywhere.[3])

My research into Ackland's life and work has emphasised to me her centrality in Warner's mind and creative vision. There is no doubt that Warner's influence, both as muse and mentor, exerted an equal and opposite force on Ackland's own work, but this essay concentrates solely on Warner's writing. Its purpose is not to examine the complex question of mutual influence between Warner and Ackland, but to trace some of the types of 'Valentinisms' Warner habitually employed, and outline their frequency and their deep significance to Warner.

In its simplest form, the Valentinism is merely a nod in her direction, an authorial tip of the nib. This may be a coded message to Ackland (who was, after all, Warner's first reader), the invocation of a place of mutual significance, or the mention of a symbolic object. The very frequency of these small nuggets of private meaning is rather touching, and they are readily identifiable. An obvious example is the gift of 'a yellow snail shell' by Thomas to Tiphaine in 'The Five Black Swans', which immediately recalls Ackland's early present to Warner of 'two small snail shells, one orange, one lemon-yellow, smelling of Valentine.'[4] This scented gift, which seemed to Warner a piece of inexplicable magic, as though nature were in league with Valentine, was one of the most potent symbols of their love-affair, which Warner mentioned frequently. Its appearance here is surely intended to symbolise Thomas's effortless dominion over the natural world and his imagination as a lover.

'The Five Black Swans' is altogether an example of a message to Valentine, every element of which is related to her. The eponymous swans were special birds in Ackland's personal iconography (swallows, falcons, even feathers, were all her symbols). Black swans signalled death – not necessarily an evil in Ackland's view - and certainly refer to her poem 'Sleep', with its lines 'And by her death I ambushed/Alone the wild black swan'. This poem haunted Warner after Ackland had died, and she believed it possibly referred to her own death[5]. There is clearly a parallel between Tiphaine, the Queen of Elfhame who has outlived her mortal lover by centuries and still mourns his loss, and Warner, who was indifferent to her longevity without Ackland. Warner's identification with Tiphaine proved strangely prescient, for – like the character in her story – she died on May Day.

More obscurely, Valentine's places of significance sometimes appear in unlikely company, where the reader might not be expecting such a connection. In 'A Scent of Roses' (the story in which a man is appalled when the prostitute he has visited regularly for years retires to get married) there are several descriptions of Norfolk, as the woman's childhood home. This 'incantation of Thurne', Warner explained, 'is a love-poem to my Love'[6]. Under Warner's authorial guidance, her lyrical Norfolk descriptions are revealed as definite communications with Valentine; they are indeed love-poems, however unlikely and irrelevant the setting.

In a more complex manner, Ackland is often present as a source of story, as the literal initiator or inspirer. It is hardly necessary to cite every instance of Warner writing in her diary some phrase equivalent to 'Began a short story on what Valentine told me'[7] to understand that she and Ackland found inspiration in each other on the literal level of exchanging stories, as well as in more profound ways. Warner used all her areas of experience as creative raw material; stories of her mother's Indian background or events of her own eccentric childhood were as useful to her as local gossip from Dorset villages or observed vignettes of wartime behaviour. She found Ackland a valuable source in this basic way, for sparks which might catch her imagination and set off a story. (This applied not only to Ackland's store of old story and procurement of gossip, but also to her wide and enthusiastic reading, from the most erudite works to grisly tabloid newspaper reports.)

'Two Children' is a late story by Warner, based on a tale told her by Ackland about a Norfolk fishing family. Three of them had been drowned, despite which the children were still allowed to play on the beach, but – though nobody in the village had ever died of snakebite – they were forbidden the heath for fear of adders. (They feared the unknown more than the lethally familiar.) Warner referred to it as 'the Winterton story'[8], and in its conjuration of Ackland's childhood summer home it is again one of the love-poems of place. It is also a story grown from a recital of local tales and types into an extraordinary portrait of human frailty and folly. An understanding of Ackland's influence extends it further, from a tale of betrayal and disillusionment to a parable of death and departure. Johnnie is the name Ackland chose for the alter ego hero of her own 'Norfolk Story'[9], and here Warner borrows it for the younger of the two children. Unlike his sister Bella he is unafraid of snakes (which were a passion of Ackland's) and strongly aware of the gender divide, which he feels gives him natural superiority. Warner delineates their relationship, their sea and countryside, and the Norfolk idiom, with her usual precision. At the end, collecting the sea's indifferent gift of wrecked oranges, Johnnie deserts Bella in her moment of great need. A dead body has been washed up on the shore, and Johnnie leaves her alone, trying to deny the death, while he makes his faithless passage to adulthood. ' "You bugger off," he said. He saw her face contort for tears, and walked on with a firm tread to join the men.'[10] Written shortly after Ackland's death, this is both a memorial to her, in terms of place and people, and also a way of speaking of her death in anger, as an abandonment.

The Mr Edom stories ('so much a part of living with Valentine'[11]) were inspired by Ackland in a lighter vein, and are full of objects of significance, The subject and its attendant wealth of detail was based on Ackland's alternative professional world of the antique trade. The business of bidding in the auction room, hunting beautiful things and triumphantly acquiring them, making valuations or dealing with a variety of eccentric customers, is all a gift to Warner's pen. The expert inside knowledge of antiques and trader's stock wisdom which Warner uses to such good effect clearly come from Ackland, as Warner was delighted to acknowledge. Writing of the proofs of *The Listening Woman* she stated the link with unusual emphasis: 'Every line of them refers back to her, or was fed by her...'[12].

The figure of Valentine appears frequently and recognisably in Warner's writing, usually in the guise of a character, but also as her named self. This personage is often manifested as tall, handsome, autocratic and apparently male. The gender discrepancy is both a private joke about Ackland's cross-dressed 'masculine' appearance, and a public statement of Warner's complicity - for those with the ability to read it. Warner was intensely proud of her lover, and her looks, and delighted in portraying her thus disguised in her real appearance. Although there is not space here for a discussion of Warner's general policy of gender disruption, the following examples of Valentine's presence at least indicate it. These striking Valentine-figures can be recognised in the breadth of Warner's writing from her early work through to the 1970s, and usually signal mischief.

The Introduction to *The Cat's Cradle Book,* written in 1940, is set very recognisably in their Norfolk home, Frankfort Manor. Ackland is cast as lord of the house, a handsome youth whose 'lock of hair fell over one eye'[13]. The narrator begins 'I had never seen a handsomer young man'; an apparently straightforward statement which is ambiguous enough to apply, perfectly literally, to Valentine. This fairytale prince is feline, and has been taught cat-language by a beautiful Siamese – who is named after Ackland's beloved Haru. His voice is 'slightly haughty, slightly distant', he has 'ownership in every inch of him', he quotes Havelock Ellis and dispenses asparagus and vin d'Anjou. He seduces the narrator effortlessly on the lawn, which, as at Frankfort, has never been cut except with a scythe.

Thus many of Ackland's traits (including a penchant for outdoor sex) are incorporated into a mocking yet admiring portrait. Warner is surely pursuing her private gender-joke and celebrating the fact that Ackland was not, in fact, a man, when she mentions that the youth has not shaved, and repeats it for emphasis: 'He was as beautiful, as elegant, as grand-mannered as yesterday, only the fine stubble blurring the outline of cheek and chin assured me that it was now today'. Warner was well aware that her private diary and letters and probably other material would be published after her death, and that Valentine would then be immediately recognisable to any reader, not just their own contemporary circle. It is not chance, surely, that in this story she mentions that a secret cultural history (that of the cats) should be placed in the British Museum with 'a Joanna Southcott-like stipulation that the seal should not be broken until the coming of a more rational age'.

The story is a sustained fantasy, which moves from dream-like beauty to macabre horror, ending with the feline plague, which wiped out the cat population of Frankfort. Its humour is curious, its happenings – like those in many of the stories which follow – mostly puzzling and unpleasant. To perceive the presence of Valentine in the person of the hero transforms the reading of it into a tribute to 'otherness', a meditation on the world's unreadiness to accept it, and a warning about the possible fate of the different in the late 1930s.

At the other end of Warner's writing life, she invoked Valentine as True Thomas, or Thomas the Rhymer, in 'The Five Black Swans' Ackland was something of a mythomane, in which she was enthusiastically aided by Warner, who hailed her as 'my light and my gravity…my more than music…my true sky…my handsome…my falcon…my sweet spouse…my lovely Lesbian' (among many other titles), and described her as a unicorn, a pirate, a mermaid, a knight, a true poet[14]. Thomas the Rhymer was a favourite alter ego of Ackland's and this story, which is so full of Valentine, can be read as a lament for her death, as well as a premonitory spell for Warner's.

True Thomas, the poet of lowland Scots legend who saw the future and could speak only the truth, was to Ackland a poet with a sacred duty like herself. In Ackland's later poetry of witness, and alarm for the state of the world, she envisaged the poet as a priestly figure whose function was to speak for the powerless and bear witness to their suffering. Her *Ballad of Thomas the Rhymer*[15] opens 'How full the rivers of Elfland run/Enough to flood the sea' and continues 'All the blood split on earth, they say,/Flows through the Elfland streams'. Her use of this legend – and the theme of Elfland – was remembered by Warner nearly thirty years later and reworked as an act of love and a continued inhabitance of their shared imaginative world.

Tiphaine first meets Thomas on May Day (one of Warner and Ackland's holy days): 'there, lolling on the grass, was a handsome man – so handsome that she checked her horse's pace to have a completer look at him'. They become lovers and 'from then on it was as though she lived to music'. The entire description of this love, of Thomas's talents and his tragic mortalness, is a meditation on Valentine – and it is incredibly poignant. It's a tribute of great brilliance and subtlety, sketching in Valentine's human faults as well as her artist's uniqueness, with love and understanding. Thus a fairytale version of their particular situation and relationship is rendered into a work of universal application on love, loss and inequality of different sorts between lovers. 'He made little of her flying, even less of her queenship, nothing at all of her immense seniority. Love was in the present…' Tiphaine's last words, centuries on, are 'Thomas – O Thomas, my love'; she is supposed to be naming her successor. Warner's moral ending, in this case, shows that true love has outlasted everything else, and is more important than status, superhuman capabilities, or even age and death; a message to Valentine, again, as well as a remarkable story.

A character actually named Valentine is introduced in 'My Shirt is in Mexico'[16], and remains carefully ungendered throughout. This apparently trivial, anecdotal story was perhaps prompted by Ackland's gift of clothes to the refugee Ludwig Renn ('Renatus Leutner') – a piece of gender confusion which would have amused Warner. Ackland's presence is not explained, her place as an intimate companion of the narrator is taken as inevitable. She is named but, as Warner knew from experience, the name was usually presumed to be masculine; no pointers in the text confirm this, nor does anything disprove it. The reader's own preconception, or foreknowledge, is delicately unstated by Warner.

There are other subtextual evidences of social disruption; the buffet car attendant who tells them the tale is obviously also gay, his innocently camp confiding manner and wish to talk to the authorial couple (whom he treats 'as though we were already friends of his') making this abundantly clear. The eponymous shirt, which he has cheerfully donated to a chance-met refugee travelling to America, becomes symbolic of a happy world of gay solidarity. Also Communism – though not openly named – is very present as a force for good; Mexico is Edenic, the waiter and passengers are on terms of absolute equality, the refugee's thank you letter speaks of a 'comrade', and those who have clothes share, quite naturally, with those who lack them.

The sartorial emphasis of the story, in which the shirt is an iconic object (a blue shirt, from London and thus 'a better style'), gently sends up Valentine the dandy. Warner wrote frequently and appreciatively about her lover's clothes, for example, 'her *shirts*, their colours: the scarlet silk, the grey and silver brocade, the cobalt blue canvas-cloth, the willow-green silk'[17]. It also celebrates a certain gay complicity between men's-shirted Valentine, able to share her masculine wardrobe with Ludwig Renn, and the waiter donating his beautiful new shirt to Renatus Leutner. There is a delicate suggestion in the letter that he and the refugee share an understanding of the potential relationships of their world: 'I do not forget the kindness. I hope you are well and make always new friends'.

As a character, this named 'Valentine' is more affable and relaxed than the handsome Valentine-figures, and Warner renders her charm with a sure hand, and great economy. Valentine only speaks twice, once to commend Mexico's Communist programme of road-building, vaccination and literacy as 'sensible beginnings', and once to agree that the waiter was lucky to have the shirt with him to give away. "You were [lucky]," said Valentine. "I can't wish anyone better luck than that."

This very short story accurately portrays Ackland's place in Warner's life; always there, always alert to her companion's wishes, sharing her humour and her fascination with people. It's surely significant that when Valentine is actually named and identified with her character there is none of Warner's usual ruthlessness with her creations, no cruel combining of the lyrical and shocking. Instead, the narrator and her 'Valentine' inhabit a world where, despite rumours of war and dispossession, comrades across the world are united in fellowship, and enjoy coffee and cake on the London to Plymouth train.

There are many variants of the Valentine figure, which become easily recognisable as soon as their presence is acknowledged. There are also, Warner being her inimitable self, occasions on which some Valentine identifiers are present, but not the whole range of characteristics. This would be less noticeable without the full presence of Valentine elsewhere, but it is evidently part of Warner's creative process of patchworking disparate elements together to create a remarkable whole.

Sophia in *Summer Will Show,* Warner's 'Lesbian novel'[18] (as Ackland and Warner privately called it), is one such. Not the instantly recognisable Valentine figure of the beautiful youth portraits, Sophia is nevertheless a relation. Her height, supercilious shyness, penchant for boxing and very English good manners are passing nods in Valentine's direction, although her superbly delineated Victorian mindset is, obviously, quite unlike. Similarly, Minna's extraordinary gift for storytelling and her world-weary ardour (both revolutionary and amatory) irresistibly conjure aspects of Warner herself, without being a portrait in other respects.

The reader who has become adept at recognising these Valentine touches will have no difficulty in identifying her mark on Satan in *Lolly Willowes* [19]. Although he doesn't have the staggering good looks of more complete portraits, Satan certainly possesses some typical Valentinisms; he is imperturbable, beautifully mannered, silkily ironical, with a 'peculiarly slow and easy' or 'prowling' gait. He is passionately devoted to the English countryside, dresses like a gamekeeper, and is a kind of natural deity or 'black knight, wandering about and succouring decayed gentlewomen'. This much seems very like one of Warner's partial Valentine tributes.

The only problem with this reading is that *Lolly Willowes* was, of course, written before Warner ever met Ackland, and several years before they became friends and then lovers. The process of borrowing characteristics in this case, therefore, happened in reverse: life imitating art. Valentine was an enthusiastic early reader of the book, and her poet's persona was a work in progress at the time; she would have been nineteen or twenty. As she became the poet Valentine, she evidently paid her mentor Warner close attention, and incorporated some of her prescriptions for satanic style.

All of these examples of Warner's work – late, early, pre-Ackland – are what might be defined as a positive view of Valentine, one which Warner stoutly upheld at all times. But there is also, surely, an echo of Ackland's self-doubt and insecurity, her fear of ageing alone and lonely without Sylvia, in some of Warner's portraits of older people. Characters such as Lucy/Aurelia in 'But at the Stroke of Midnight', or Sibyl in *The Music at Long Verney,* with their gallant pride and immense frailty, are captured in some of Warner's most painful and terrifying writing. She did not scruple to borrow from life incidents such as Ackland's car-crash, although she put the world to rights by allowing Sibyl to win the ensuing case. ('She had always been a good driver, was still a good driver, but she was unequipped for a generation of bad drivers'.[20]) And this charm worked, too; Valentine did not share their fate.

Clearly, Warner was prepared to use incidents from Ackland's life – or, more precisely, their shared life – in an apparently ruthless manner. She used herself in the same way; it was part of her absolute dedication to her work. Ackland seems to have accepted this situation completely, and held a corresponding attitude in relation to her own poetry. However, with Warner's poetry, rather than fiction, there are instances of Ackland being distressed by its public pronouncement of their private emotions. *Lost Summer*, a cycle of poems by Warner about Ackland's infidelity, was set to music by Paul Nordoff; hearing it made Ackland consider suicide[21]. Of its nature, some of the poetry has a more directly obvious link to the author's life, but Warner's poetry is as diverse as her fiction. The same alertness for the presence of Valentine in the poetry will often make for rewarding reading, for apart from the love-poems, in which Warner is obviously going to invoke her, she appears by influence or inference in other sorts of poem too. There is only space here for one brief example; in 'Earl Cassilis's Lady', one of Warner's beautiful variations on a folksong theme, the wife who has run off with the gipsies says 'I was tall,/Silken and made for love…', a phrase Warner quoted about Ackland, and her infidelity[22].

The presence of Valentine is also apprehended in Warner's work in another way, because of the shared intellectual landscape which they jointly inhabited, holding whole areas of the imagination in common. As a result, there are certain recurring motifs present in both writers' work, themes of mutual interest, and – most often and most elusively – a certain tone or ethos in Warner's writing which suggests the inspiration of Valentine's presence. The importance for both writers of this joint 'country of the mind'[23] can be gauged by the distress Warner felt when she believed Ackland had strayed into another, alien land by becoming a Catholic[24]. Ackland, in her turn, was devastated to be sent into intellectual exile as a result.

In certain specific ways Warner and Ackland had similar backgrounds; both were proud of their Scottish blood, yet profoundly English, both thought of London as home, both had youthful success in artistic circles, Warner in Bloomsbury and Ackland in Fitzrovia. Thus particular concepts – the idea of the North, Scottish fairytales, English folk art and traditions, pastoral poetry, Bohemian living, a strong awareness of people in history – were to them not only joint creative stock, but also an almost familial connection. The same is true of certain images which are used repeatedly by both writers – the river, the moon, the all-important landscape, gardens and growing things, animals especially cats. Warner makes these motifs reappear in her stories with the familiarity of home; they are used similarly in Ackland's poems.

Warner's choice of subject-matter can often be directly traced to Ackland beginnings in terms of its political and social content. Although she was by nature a believer in liberty and human rights, and a critic of capitalism and Empire, Warner always made clear that her conversion to active political involvement came about through Ackland[25]. Her political writing, as well as being the result of deep conviction, was thus a tribute to Ackland, on whom she could rely to apply Marxist theory to *The Corner that Held Them*, or relate *After the Death of Don Juan* to the Communist struggle. Her care to write about apparently 'ordinary' people, particularly during the war, is doubtless part of this commitment to write as a worker – and their frequent descents into eccentricity accurately reflect Warner's highly individualistic take on Communism.

Just as the left-wing action instigated by Ackland on a practical level soon found expression in Warner's work, so did the physical relationship initiated by her. It was not Warner's style to write fiction explicitly about lesbianism (any more than 'about' Communism, or certainly not in the contemporary realist sense employed by many of her fellow-travellers). But, like Communism, it was not absent from her work. In her poetry she chose to write openly on the theme of lesbian love doubtless because, paradoxically, the form meant she could be more specific without endangering her own sense of subtlety, just as she could write a more obviously political poem[26]. Her fiction, however, is undoubtedly lesbian in the sense that it consistently challenges a patriarchal, phallocentric world view, and presents alternative love-objects as valid and valuable[27]. *Summer Will Show* demonstrates this in its portrayal of an unconventional love relationship between women, which is so far from overt that its lesbian interpretation can be challenged – though not very convincingly. From *Lolly Willowes*, the fantastical version of a feminist manifesto, to *The Flint Anchor*, with its grim indictment of patriarchy and the nuclear family, Warner never wavered in her intense criticism of manmade society. In other words, she naturally connected her personal and political lives, with the result that she occupied a political position which acknowledged her lesbianism, and feminism, as well as her communism. (That this political place was then unofficial and unnamed is another indication of Warner's independent spirit; but she was not alone there.) The presence of Valentine in her work is one way in which Warner represented the possibility of an alternative society; the revolutionary ideal as she was actually living it.

The ways in which Warner chose to conjure the presence of Valentine are overlapping, repeated and diverse, cross-referential, obvious and obscure, infinitely varied. In 1956 Ackland wrote, 'I think it may be that in Sylvia's work I have sometimes some seed of myself sown'[28]. Her characteristic modest hesitation is contrasted by the equally characteristic dual imagery of growing to harvest or sexual impregnation. Both these readings are appropriate to Ackland's role as she saw it. She believed in her sacred trust to nurture Warner's genius, to tend that garden in the domestic sense, rather like the artist's helpmeet who would, inevitably, be the wife in a heterosexual relationship. (Thus their roles were reversed, in the perception of those who presumed to cast Ackland as the 'husband' because of her perceived masculinity. Their relationship altogether confounded those who tried to view it as a marriage in the binary male/female sense; although they were happy to talk of each other as a spouse, their 'marriage' did not carry the usual range of contemporary heterosexual connotations.) Ackland thus had no conceptual difficulty in holding, simultaneously, a strong belief in her poetic potency and ability to fecundate creativity, which here seems to extend to encompass the idea of being able to fertilise Warner's work – at least sometimes. This is a masculine image, perhaps, but it reflects Ackland's view that insemination – despite its importance – is only the first stage in a long process towards the birth of a living creation. (Indeed, this dual image rather neatly illustrates Ackland's gender policy, which was to usurp masculinity to her own uses as a woman.)

It is, at all events, a belief in her contribution with which Warner would have had no quarrel[29]. She practised the presence of Valentine, as we have seen, in all forms of her writing, at all periods of her work. Before and after Ackland's death, there is surprisingly little difference in these evocations, since Ackland evidently remained vividly alive in Warner's mind. The element of conjuration increases in its intensity, and there is a poignance (for the reader) in the encoded greetings meant for Valentine, but the same basic elements are present at all times. No doubt to write of Valentine after her death gave Warner comfort, the sense she wrote of as 'My mind, my consciousness, safe in her arms'[30]. But even before her loss of the daily presence of Valentine, it was Warner's pleasure to evoke it in her work.

The practice of the presence of Valentine, in all its various forms, was an important strategy of Warner's, a confidence and joke shared with her readers, a tribute to her Valentine, and a favoured glimpse of her own very particular way of viewing the world. To realise this provides insight into the sleight of hand whereby she transformed the material of her life, by creative alchemy, into her unparalleled work. Warner was, among other concerns, writing for a posterity of later readers who would be part of 'the more rational age' she anticipated. Her intent was, surely, not only to give her lover a measure of immortality (or even a share in her creative offspring), but also to inform us – the suitably enlightened products of this more rational age – of her dedication to a life of love, a revolutionary relationship. Warner was intensely proud of that unconventional relationship, and she emphasises the important contribution which it made to her art, and its political aspect. It was undoubtedly part of Warner's design that, far from being marginalised, Valentine Ackland would be recognised as a central figure, ever-present in her lover's text as she was in her life.

Frances Bingham is a freelance writer.

Notes

[1] *The Practice of the Presence of God*, Nicholas Herman, 1692/STW diary 22 May 1970

[2] *The Diaries of Sylvia Townsend Warner*, ed. Claire Harman, Chatto & Windus, 1994; *For Sylvia: An Honest Account,* Valentine Ackland, Chatto & Windus, 1985 *I'll Stand By You: The Letters of Sylvia Townsend Warner and Valentine Ackland,* ed. Susanna Pinney, Pimlico, 1988.

[3] See: *The Apparitional Lesbian*, Terry Castle, Columbia University Press, 1993

[4] STW diary 16 October 1930

[5] STW diary 24 May 1971

[6] STW diary 31 July 1972

[7] STW diary 17 June 1942

[8] STW diary 24 February 1970

[9] VA, unpublished novel, Warner/Ackland archive Dorset County Museum.

[10] STW, in *The Innocent and the Guilty*, Chatto & Windus, 1971.

[11] STW letter to William Maxwell, 18 January, 1971.

[12] STW diary 12 January 1971.

[13] *The Cat's Cradle Book*, Chatto & Windus, 1960. As Wendy Mulford notes, this forelock is one of Valentine's most mentioned features. *This Narrow Place – Sylvia Townsend Warner and Valentine Ackland: Life, Letters and Politics 1930-1951,* Pandora, 1988.

[14] STW letters and poems to VA: see notes 2 and 26.

[15] Valentine Ackland, *New Republic*, 1942.

[16] *A Garland of Straw*, Chatto & Windus, 1943.

[17] STW diary 30 September 1970.

[18] VA diary 16 May 1932.

[19] *Lolly Willowes*, Chatto & Windus, 1926.

[20] *The Music at Long Verney*, The Harvill Press, 2001

[21] . VA diary 16 May 1952, and an unpublished short story May 16th in a Diary, in which the song-cycle is called 'Time Spent'.

[22] STW, 'Earl Cassilis's Lady', *Twelve Poems*, Chatto& Windus, 1980/STW diary 13 August 1970.

[23] 'When I Have Said I Love You', VA, *The Nature of the Moment,* Chatto and Windus, 1973.

[24] 'Briefly, Sylvia minds violently and deeply', VA diary 1 March 1956.

[25] STW narrative 6 in *I'll Stand by You*.

[26] See STW's poems in *Whether a Dove or Seagull*, such as 'Drawing you heavy with sleep'.

[27] See *Mr Fortune's Maggot*, 'A Love Match', 'The True Heart', 'Some World Far From Ours', etc, etc.

[28] VA diary Easter Sunday 1956.

[29] 'We shall be remembered together', she wrote. STW diary 25 February 1970.

[30] STW diary 20 January 1971.

(Unpublished works, and diary entries which are not printed, are all from the Warner/Ackland archive in Dorset County Museum).

CHAPTER 3

On the Compositional Genetics of the *Kingdoms of Elfin* together with a Note on Tortoises

John Simons

> "If you don't want to offend the Queen, dress yourself properly and hurry back. What's wrong with your werewolves? Moulting?"
> "Dying."
> "That won't do you any good. I daresay they won't all die. I'm sure old Duke Billy won't. Bet you a hundred Duke Billy won't die."

This exchange between Aquilon, Master of the Royal Pack of Werewolves at the fairy court of Brocéliande and his cousin Beliard takes place in the middle of Sylvia Townsend Warner's story 'The Mortal Milk' one of the sequence of tales some of which were first published in the *New Yorker* and which were subsequently collected as a separate volume.[1] The interesting thing about this little snatch of conversation is the casual naming of one of the ailing werewolves as Duke Billy. Who is Duke Billy?

The answer is to be found in the corpus of Middle English romances. Duke Billy is, undoubtedly, Duke William of Palerne the protagonist of a Middle English poem produced in the East Midlands some time in the middle of the fourteenth century and existing in one manuscript that can be dated to between 1360 and 1375. Like most of the Middle English romances *William of Palerne* is a translation of a much older French text dating from c. 1194 – 1197 and produced for Yolande of Hainaut, Countess of St Pol. In the original texts William is not himself a werewolf but is rescued from the plotting of his wicked uncle by a friendly werewolf (who later, in the engaging way of presenting the marvellous as commonplace so typical of the Middle English romances, turns out to be Prince Alphouns of Spain) and eventually redeems his inheritance, the Kingdom of Sicily, Apulia and Calabria. The Old French text also seems to contain elements of another Old French werewolf tale, the *lai* of *Bisclavret*, which was composed, also in the late twelfth century, by Marie de France. Marie almost certainly lived and worked in England and claimed that her poems were derived from old Breton tales.

Now, setting aside the minor inaccuracy in referring to Duke Billy as a werewolf, I think that Townsend Warner clearly was drawing on a medieval source for this otherwise rather puzzling passage. Although the *Kingdoms of Elfin* stories were written in the 1960s and 1970s when authors could still expect a reasonable level of general education from their readers the use of a text such a *William of Palerne* to tell a joke is still pretty obscure. Elsewhere in the *Kingdoms of Elfin* Townsend Warner makes explicit reference to medieval texts - in 'The Revolt at Brocéliande', for example, she cites the Old French poet Wace (she refers to him as Norman although he was, in fact, based in Jersey) who spoke of his desire to visit the forest of Brocéliande, which was a famous fairy kingdom in Brittany – but in the case of Duke Billy the reference is far more oblique. Indeed, it is oblique to the point of being incomprehensible to most readers.

This small textual detail was so intriguing to me when I first read the *Kingdoms of Elfin* stories that in pursuing a critical account of them I thought that it might be of interest to treat them as I might treat a medieval or early modern text and to attempt to put together the matrix of sources and influences from which they appear to derive. When these lines of influence have been teased out it ought then be possible to come to some kind of critical conclusion as to the rationale for their selection and their significance in determining the overall shape and style of the *Kingdoms of Elfin* stories. In order to do this I shall first identify the sources, then treat each in turn showing how it has contributed to the final form of Townsend Warner's collection and then, finally, show how the coming together has enabled the creation of a new text and a new kind of work.

I believe that in working on her stories Townsend Warner had three major lines of influence in mind. The first is the long passage 'On the Fairies of Popular Superstition' which functions as an introduction to 'The Tale of Tamlane' in Sir Walter Scott's *Minstrelsy of the Scottish Border*. The second are the *lais* of Marie de France. The third are the *contes de fées* of the *salon* writers of late seventeenth and early eighteenth-century France and, possibly, the corresponding but slightly earlier literary folk tales of Italy.

One very obvious feature of the *Kingdoms of Elfin* is Townsend Warner's consistent attempt to construct a kind of typology of fairies. Her stories move between different fairy lands and we encounter a number of different kinds of supernatural beings, all with their own attributes and all with their own distinctive cultures. Indeed, Townsend Warner often appears to spend as much time on the loving reconstruction of the fine detail of fairy ritual and material culture as she does on the pursuit of the twists and turns of her narratives. This offers the reader a different experience from the usual expectation of this kind of story and grounds the fairies in a reality that is every bit as rich and realised as that in Townsend Warner's more conventional novels and short fictions. Referring to one story, she pointed out in a letter to Marchette and Joy Chute:

> It...has a great deal of information about Elfhame unknown till now as I have just invented it. Oh, how I long to give it learned footnotes, and references. There is such heartless happiness in scholarship.[2]

The current study is, to some extent, a reconstruction of what those footnotes might have been.

Scott's essay is designed to offer a full account of the varieties of the world of folk tradition.[3] Scott introduces us, *inter alia*, to elves, Froddenskenten (from Lapland), fairies, Peris, water spirits, and the various Celtic names for the little people. By doing this in the context of the rich complex of regional and international traditions concerning the properties and behaviours of these different kinds of supernatural beings Scott provides the reader with an quasi-anthropological account of the Other World. In order to achieve this Scott draws on a number of sources, some of which he explores in considerable detail. The most important for our purposes are the folk beliefs of Scotland and the Middle English romance of *Sir Orfeo*, a re-telling of the myth of Orpheus and Euridice set in a fairy world near Winchester (the modern name for Thrace as the poet helpfully explains) and explicitly referred to by the author as a Breton *lai*.

In fact, a number of the stories in *Kingdoms of Elfin* are set in Scotland, which thus becomes the collection's most fully realised location in the mortal world. *Minstrelsy of the Scottish Border* brought together key themes in Romanticism, the 'Scotch songs' of the Augustans, and the Gothic with serious philological and antiquarian study and was one of the most influential books of the nineteenth century occupying much the same place as Bishop Thomas Percy's *Reliques of Ancient English Poetry* had held in the eighteenth. It also looked forward to the Victorian 'discovery' of the Borders and Highlands. It is not conceivable that a woman of Townsend Warner's age and social class would have been ignorant of Scott's book. So even if we did not accept that it was the powerful pressure of Scott's introduction that led Townsend Warner to her typological and classificatory approach we might still see it as offering her a stimulus to place her tales.

To be more precise, six out of sixteen of the stories have Scottish locations and these locations seem quite carefully and deliberately located in a world made familiar by Scott. In 'The Occupation', for example, a Manse is taken over by fairies whose mischief drives the Calvinist minister – who tries to make sense of things by reading a seventeenth-century Scottish treatise on 'The Secret Commonwealth' – into insanity and the damnation of losing his faith.

This detail of 'The Secret Commonwealth' is quite interesting and gives us an insight into the kind of scholarly game that Townsend Warner was enjoying in the composition of her collection of stories. We can date the story's fictive world quite precisely from a reference to 'Jamie Hogg the shepherd'. This is, of course, James Hogg the 'Ettrick Shepherd' who was lionised by the literary establishment as a genuine peasant writer. Between 1777 and the 1790s Hogg was still working as a shepherd so this gives a time period for the events of the story. Townsend Warner is quite precise in saying that the minister is reading a manuscript of the Reverend Robert Kirk's *The Secret Commonwealth* and dates that manuscript to 1691. Robert Kirk is an interesting figure in himself and occupies his own place in Scottish folklore but it is of some significance that Townsend Warner specifies that her minister is reading a manuscript of his work. No early printed version of Kirk's text is known and it was first published in Edinburgh in 1815 (i.e. after the dates set for Townsend Warner's story). However, in his 1830 *Letters on Demonology and Witchcraft*, Sir Walter Scott claims that there was a printed version of Kirk's text dating from 1691. If Townsend Warner had got her knowledge of Kirk solely from Scott she might have been tempted to have her character reading a printed text. In 1893 Andrew Lang, the Victorian folklorist and author of fairy tales, edited Kirk's text and made it quite clear that there was no 1691 print or, if there was, it so scarce as to have vanished and casts doubt on Scott's claim that such a book ever existed. It therefore appears likely that Townsend Warner derived some of her knowledge of Kirk's treatise from Lang and thus, by carefully dating her story and scrupulously stressing that the book was in the Manse only in manuscript, she embeds a neat little scholarly joke.

In 'Foxcastle', a scholarly young lecturer in Rhetoric at Glasgow University wanders in pursuit of his philological studies into a fairy barrow where he is kept prisoner for decades without understanding that time has passed. In 'The One and the Other', Adam, an aristocratic elf who has been exchanged at birth with the Queen's mortal favourite Tiffany, wanders through the Borders making a living by showing his credentials from the Dollar University. In 'The Five Black Swans' Queen Tiphaine of the Scottish Kingdom of Elfhame dies broken hearted after her sexual encounter with the legendary poet and seer

Thomas of Ercildoune. This is an incident taken direct from Scott who made his own additions to the traditional ballad and also wrote about Thomas in the *Letters on Witchcraft and Demonology* as well as in *Minstrelsy of the Scottish Border*.

In these Scottish tales Townsend Warner is clearly playing with the categories, ideas and settings she derives from Scott. But her use of Scott is also transformative. Where in the essay 'On the Fairies of Popular Superstition' a few sentences suffice to describe a particular fairy attribute Townsend Warner will devise a whole story around it. Where, in one of Scott's novels a character such as James Sutherland in 'Foxcastle' will be drawn over perhaps a hundred pages or the breakdown of Minister Gideon Baxter in 'The Occupation' might form a three-decker novel, in Townsend Warner these processes are condensed into a psychologically intense but whimsical short narrative.

I have already suggested that Townsend Warner would have been alerted to the potential of the Breton *lais* through Scott's essay although her clear knowledge of a relatively obscure text such as *William of Palerne* demonstrates the kind of familiarity with medieval culture that might be expected from someone who spent the first period of their adult life as a serious and influential academic historian of Tudor church music. As I have remarked above Townsend Warner makes specific reference to Wace and, by the late nineteenth century, the influence of Wace's *Brut* on at least some of Marie de France's *lais* had been well established. So if Townsend Warner had studied Wace even superficially she may well have come across the thread of scholarship that would have taken her from the high seriousness of Wace's historiographic epic to the lighter, lyrical world of Marie de France's short poems.[4]

Marie's *lais* are characterised by their concise and supernaturally driven narratives. The conceit is always that the stories derive from the Bretons. So there is a Celtic connection, although what this claim actually means is debatable. The Middle Breton poetry that has survived is largely of a devotional character (although there is evidence for a now lost corpus of secular Arthurian stories) so if Marie was basing her *lais* on Breton sources these have either disappeared or were available to her through oral sources only. In fact, if Marie was working from traditional story material she modifies it greatly by casting the fairy world of the early Celts in the cultural mode of *amour courtoise* derived from the courts of Provence and only just becoming familiar in northern France and England during her lifetime. The Breton connection may, of course, be simply a literary flourish designed to give an exotic setting to her poems. By the fourteenth century, the Breton *lai* had become a genre in its own right and poets such as Thomas Chestre (probably author of *Sir Launfal*, a version of Marie de France's *Lanval*), the anonymous author of *Sir Orfeo*, or Chaucer in *The Franklin's Tale* certainly had no connection with Bretons but still claimed them as the sources of their stories. In addition, there has to be the question as to whether Bretons actually means Britons (i.e. Welsh) and nobody today doubts that although too much credibility cannot be placed in the idea of fully-formed Arthurian epics in Middle Welsh it is still highly probable that Arthurian story material came into the world of Anglo-Norman and Old French chivalry through the Norman baronial courts of the Welsh Marches. Interestingly though, Townsend Warner does make a specific reference to Breton folk tale in a letter composed at about the time when the *Kingdoms of Elfin* were starting to form in her mind.[5]

Only one of Townsend Warner's stories ('Visitors to a Castle') has a Welsh setting – and a humourously down at heel setting it is too. So one could not claim, as one can for the relationship with Scott, that any influence on Kingdoms of Elfin from the Breton *lais* is pervasively present in the collection. However, it could be argued that the ethos of the *lais* pervades Townsend Warner's texts most intensively. Marie de France's *lais* are, in some ways, the closest things to short stories that the Middle Ages has to offer us. There is a concentration on just one or maybe two main characters. The stories usually revolve around the dilemmas set by love. Both of these characteristics are reflected in most of the stories in the *Kingdoms of Elfin*. In addition, while Marie's appropriation of a supposed traditional Breton culture gives her tales the appearance of ancient derivation their articulation of traditional material (if it really is there) with up-to-date theories of courtly behaviour must have made her poems appear strikingly modern to the court of Henry II where they were probably first read.

Again, Townsend Warner's stories have the same double focus. On the one hand, there is the traditional fairy material drawn either from earlier sources or simply made up. On the other, the fairies are absolutely contemporary in their language, morals and *mores*. On occasion, the reader is brought up short by the incursion of a modern incident from the human world which, in *Kingdoms of Elfin,* is always dimly seen as running parallel to the supernatural as a place to observe, visit or steal from. In 'Visitors to a Castle' for instance, the fairies give first aid to the District Nurse who has fallen from her bicycle. Thus, while it is not as easy to attribute a very direct influence of Marie de France and the Breton *lais* on Townsend Warner as it was to discern and identify the broad influence of Scott, it is easy to show how the ethos and some structural features of the medieval texts might have acted as a general guide to her thinking as she formed an overall sense of the kind of stories she was planning to write.

In 1550-1553 the Venetian Giovan Francesco Straparola published *Le Piacevoli Notti* and when this drew the unwelcome and dangerous attention of the Inquisition he defended himself by claiming that all he was doing was harmlessly recording the innocent traditional stories that he had heard told by the city's women. A few decades (1634-1636) later the Neapolitan Giambattista Basile wrote *Il Pentamerone*. This was also, allegedly, based on traditional tales (including early versions of Sleeping Beauty and Cinderella). However, whatever the real sources of Straparola's and Basile's texts, both authors had a common purpose and this was to develop their tales into sophisticated, erotic and courtly confections intended to delight a well-to-do audience whose lives were far removed from the slums and villages of the peasant story tellers from whom they may, or may not, have been collected. The other thing that these two collections have in common is that while they are written by a male author the claim is that they are stories originally told by women or have female narrators.[6]

The influence of these stories, and of Basile's collection in particular, was felt most immediately in France. Although Charles Perrault's *Les Contes de Ma Mère l'Oyle* (1697) is now the best-remembered collection of the French vogue for *salon* fairy tales Perrault by no means originated the genre. From 1685 onwards Madame Marie-Catherine d'Aulnoy had been telling stories in her *salon* and collected them in writing in 1690. Her follower, the lively (she was banished to the Chateau of Loche for her unconventional behaviour and alleged lesbianism) Henriette-Julie de Castenau, Comtesse de Murat also wrote and published fairy tales. Marie-Jeanne de l'Héritier, a protegée of the famous Madeleine de Scudery, was likewise a writer of fairy tales and she had her own follower in Catherine Bernard. Another important writer of fairy tales at the time was Mlle de la Force.[7]

These *salon* tales grew out of the conversational parlour games of the Parisian *précieuses* and, as such, constitute an unusual literary genre. They weave the traditional stories of the French countryside (which the aristocratic *salonières* would very probably have heard from their nurses) with humourous and erotic incident and convert the direct vernacular speech of the originals into a rarefied Rococo dialect far removed from anything that they may have heard in the nursery. Although there were men who formed part of this literary movement – the Chevalier de Mailly and Jean de Préchac are examples of male disciples of Perrault – the main impetus came from women and this was continued in the next century by Mlle de Lubert, Mme de Villeneuve and Mme Leprince de Beaumont who, like Marie de France, worked in England.

In addition to the stories derived from traditional French folk tale the salons generated an interest in Oriental tales which was first stimulated by Antoine Galland's translation of *The Thousand and One Nights* (1704 – 1717) and which remained a vogue into the early nineteenth century. Perhaps Voltaire's *Candide,* Johnson's *Rasselas*, and Beckford's *Vathek* remain the best-known, if heavily ironised in the first two cases, examples of this craze.[8]

The *Kingdoms of Elfin* bear clear traces of the influence of these kinds of stories. It has been observed that the stories make use of themes from the French stories in the same way as do the narratives in Angela Carter's *The Bloody Chamber* but I think that this is probably because of the common cores of story material used by Townsend Warner and her French ancestresses.[9] What is clear, however, is that Townsend Warner's stories pick up key generic markers from the *précieuses*. These include the consistently erotic charge of some of the stories and the wit and intelligence that transforms traditional material, often associated with children, into entertainment for a sophisticated adult reader.

But Townsend Warner does provide us with a full-blown version of an Oriental tale. 'The Search for an Ancestress' tells of the visit of Joost, a fairy from the Elfin Court of Zuy (it is made amusingly clear that compared with the sophisticated French world of Brocéliande the down-to-earth Dutch world of Zuy is a pretty poor affair), to the Persian Kingdom of the Peris. Sir Walter Scott made the point that the Norman and Breton tales are influenced by the Eastern traditions of the Peris but, although Townsend Warner could have derived the idea for 'The Search for an Ancestress' from Scott, it is also highly likely that she drew on the complex of French Rococo Orientalism to build the detail and ethos of the story. Although there is always a certain brutality in the fairy world the Kingdom Joost encounters in Persia takes the casual or ritualised violence of European fairies towards each other and towards their mortal neighbours into a realm of eroticised sadism complete with that staple of Orientalist pornography the beautiful lady-in-waiting - whose throat is cut as a punishment for the crime of allowing the Queen's favourite Persian cat to climb from the Queen's lap onto her own. This story is quite unlike any other in *Kingdoms of Elfin* and it is as if Townsend Warner wished to pay full tribute to her own ancestresses by ensuring that at least one of her own stories borrowed much more than generalities from their work.

There is one tale that represents a hybrid between a French *conte* and an Oriental tale and this is 'The Blameless Triangle'. In this three elves from the Austrian court of Wirre Gedanken set themselves up as *philosophes* and, after various adventures find themselves attached to an Ottoman court somewhere in the Balkans. Two of the elves eventually return to Austria but one, Ludo, becomes the favourite of the provincial governor Mustafa Ibrahim and lives with him until he dies before setting up home in Venice where he becomes Mustafa's biographer. This is a lighter story than 'The Search for an Ancestress' but it still carries an erotic charge that was explicitly discussed by Townsend Warner in one of her letters to David Garnett:

> No, I don't mention homosexuality. Even if I had known that Irish fairies are pederasts, I doubt if I would have gone to the Kingdom of Nephin to explore for it – though in the first version of 'The Blameless Triangle' Mustafa buggered the lot, with no ill-feeling on anyone's part.[10]

This original version obviously caused a good deal of disquiet at the *New Yorker*. In a letter to her long-time friend and editor William Maxwell, Townsend Warner was moved to exclaim:

> Dear me about the buggery. Surely whatever Mr Shawn [editor of the *New Yorker*] has to say about it he must have said many times already? I can't believe (I'd like to) that I in my extreme respectable old age am the first person to pose the problem. If I am, may I have a commemorative plaque in your office please?[11]

But it is interesting to note that Townsend Warner did, in the end, suppress the overt articulation of homosexual encounters in this earlier version of this story. However, we do see something of her method of working as she then preferred instead to rely on arch implication and, of course, her readers' knowledge of the customs of Ottoman provincial courts. Here again she is, arguably, drawing not so much on a true history of the Turkish Yoke as on the fantasies of Enlightenment Orientalism as they came through her source material.

Having reviewed the lines of influence that went into the making of *Kingdoms of Elfin* we may now consider what, if any, significance they have beyond providing inspiration and stimulation. When Warner was writing these stories in the 1960s and 1970s she was becoming elderly and was wracked with grief and consequent disengagement from the world following the death, in 1969, of her long-time companion and lover Valentine Ackland. Nevertheless, she was working on the Viking Press paperback edition of *Kingdoms of Elfin* in March 1977 only ten months before her passing away at the age of 84 in January 1978.[12] In some ways *Kingdoms of Elfin* does speak to its period. There was a vogue for all things fay. The Tolkien cult was just coming into its full stride and popular editions of earlier fantasy writers like Lord Dunsanay and E. R Eddison were making their appearance together with reprints of the romances of William Morris. The free and easy world of the fairies fitted in well to a world coloured in by the dark plums and greens of Biba or the acid yellows and turquoises of Pucci. It is not hard to see the court of Elfhame as the court of Mick Jagger. But although, in this sense, Kingdoms of Elfin may be read as that dreadful thing "a book of its time" this contemporary flavour does not help us to account for its underlying influences.

To understand these, I think that we have to look further back into the world of the Victorian children's tales that Townsend Warner would have known in her own childhood. I am not talking here necessarily of the ambiguously directed stories of Oscar Wilde or the Yellow Book aestheticism which also drew on materials drawn from eighteenth-century France. I am instead thinking about the more mainstream Victorian fairy world represented by the fairy books of Andrew Lang or the verse of William Allingham.[13] Although these authors do not shake off the darkness that always shadows fairy tales they do, nonetheless, offer often moralised or prettified accounts of the savage world of traditional fairy lore. In Jack Zipes' words they:

> conceived plots conventionally to reconcile themselves and their readers to the status quo of Victorian society. Their imaginative worlds could be called exercise in complicity with the traditional opponents of fairy tales, for there is rarely a hint of social criticism and subversion in their works.[14]

In going back to medieval sources and in reading Sir Walter Scott through the lens of, say, the Comtesse de Murat, Townsend Warner is subverting the improving and protective impulses of the Victorian writers while developing a voice that is absolutely contemporary. *The Kingdoms of Elfin* stories are of their time but they are of their time because they constitute a systematic attempt to undermine the morals of the Victorian versions of similar narratives. This attempt is possible because of the marshalling of source material, which, in itself, offers a thoroughgoing asymmetry with the world of the late nineteenth century. It is also the case that this asymmetry is driven by a rereading of the medievalism that is a central facet of what we now consider Victorian style. Perhaps an interesting slip in one of Townsend Warner's letters helps us to understand how her imaginative world was bordered by the Middle Ages and the eighteenth century:

> The dinner was in the Hogarth Room, panelled with 18th cent. Portraits looking on at our 12th cent. selves.[15]

A Note on Tortoises

In 1946 Townsend Warner wrote *The Portrait of a Tortoise*.[16] This is an edited selection of those passages from Gilbert White's Journals and Letters that refer to the pet tortoise, Timothy, which he acquired from Mrs Rebecca Snooke in 1780 (although White and Timothy had been friends for several years before that) and which died in 1794 just a year after White himself. This little book is explicitly referred to as a biography and in writing it Townsend Warner was making a contribution to testudinal life-writing a miniscule but not singular genre of English letters.[17] To the best of my knowledge *The Portrait of a Tortoise* has not attracted critical attention before although I believe that it was read on B.B.C. Radio 3 some time in the late 1970s.

Although the book consists largely of extracts from White it also contains an introduction in which Townsend Warner both contextualises the place of Timothy in White's life and studies and speculates on unknown aspects of Timothy's life. This she does with a degree of high seriousness which, I believe, is not entirely designed as ironic whimsy. Timothy is treated with the same respect as a human subject and his interactions with the cherishably named Mrs Snooke, Gilbert White and White's various relations, servants and gardeners are dealt with in a way that does not make the fact that Timothy was a tortoise of any special significance. Townsend Warner does, to some extent, take a lead from White himself here who certainly seems to have seen Timothy as another member of the household (her refers to him as a 'domestic' in a letter to his niece Mary White). Gilbert also wrote anthropomorphising letters in Timothy's name to a young lady called Miss Heckey Mulso (the names of White's circle might have kept Dickens beyond the need for invention for years).

But although the treatment of Timothy as something more than an animal grows from Townsend Warner's primary source in White I believe that in her approach to writing about him she goes one step further. What the approach to Timothy in *The Portrait of a Tortoise* seems to demonstrate is the democratising tendency of Townsend Warner's world view. Her Communism - which resulted in the *longeurs* of the Parisian scenes of *Summer Will Show* and, as late as 1961, still enabled her to reflect, astonishingly to us now, on Stalin when he was neither 'mad nor bad' (this supposed Golden Age was 1941 by which time Stalin had already accounted for several million Soviet citizens) - did at least, however misguided, not lead her to that strangely nauseating egalitarianism that one finds in the upper middle class socialists of the 1930s. This is clearly shown by the fact that her hope for the discrediting of Margaret Thatcher in the mid 1970s revolved around the possibility that she might one day be caught eating asparagus with a knife and fork[18] Her sexuality too, I believe, led her to a certain kind of non-judgemental vision (very different from the bullying postures of Radclyffe Hall) that is both engaging and fragile. The promotion of Timothy's life as worth inspection in its own right seems therefore to offer itself to the reader as an exotic and unexpected product of the twentieth century's obsession with the lionisation of mass murderers on the one hand and the more genial realisation that human beings should be free to live without condemnation on the other. For this last reason *The Portrait of a Tortoise* deserves our attention.

beings should be free to live without condemnation on the other. For this last reason *The Portrait of a Tortoise* deserves our attention.

University of Lincoln

Notes

[1] All references to the *Kingdoms of Elfin* are to the Penguin Books edition (Harmondsworth, 1979).

[2] Letter to Marchette and Joy Chute 8th April, 1973. William Maxwell (ed.), *Sylvia Townsend Warner Letters* (London: Chatto and Windus, 1982), pp. 265-266.

[3] The standard edition of Scott's work is that of T. F. Henderson, 4 volumes (Edinburgh, 1932).

[4] A convenient translation of Marie de France is that of G. S. Burgess and K. Busby, *The Lais of Marie de France* (London: Penguin Books Ltd., 1986). The easiest available edition of the Old French is that of A. Ewart, *Marie de France: Lais* (Oxford: Blackwell, 1944).

[5] Letter to William Maxwell, 19th November, 1971 in Maxwell, op. cit., p. 254. The early Breton tradition first came into mainline European consciousness through the publication in 1839 of Theodore de la Vilemarqué's (known as Kervarker) Barsaz Breiz although this, like many similar collections of this time, is a highly literary production and permeated by Kervarker's knowledge of the Welsh tradition. There is also the tradition of the manuscript brought back from Brittany by Walter Calenius of Oxford in the early twelfth century and reputed to contain Arthurian material.

[6] Two excellent general works on fairy tales that contain valuable critical studies of these Italian collections are M. Warner, *From the Beast to the Blonde* (London, Chatto and Windus, 1994) and J. Zipes, *When Dreams Came True* (London: Routledge, 1999). However, it is also worth referring the interested reader to Italo Calvino's wonderful retelling of many of these tales in his *Italian Folktales* (Harmondsworth: Penguin Books, 1982).

[7] See Warner and Zipes, op. cit., for studies of these works and for a collection of translations J. Zipes, *Beauties, Beasts and Enchantments* (New York: Meridian, 1991). Some of these French *salon* tales drew on Breton traditional material, which brings the circle of influence round again to Marie de France.

[8] For a recent edition of other British tales in this genre see R. Mack, *Oriental Tales* (Oxford, Oxford University Press, 1992).

[9] By Terri Windling in *Women and Fairy Tales* (available at http://www.endicott-studio.com.rdrm/forwmnft.html

[10] Letter to David Garnett, 31st May, 1977. In Maxwell, op. cit., p. 296.

[11] Letter of William Maxwell, 19th October, 1973. In Maxwell, op. cit., p. 270.

[12] See C. Harman, (ed.), *The Diaries of Sylvia Townsend Warner* (London: Virago, 1995).

[13] Material on these can be found in Warner op. cit. and Zipes, *When Dreams Came True*, pp. 111 - 140. See also K. M. Briggs, *The Fairies in Tradition and Literature* London, Routledge and

Kegan Paul, 1967), pp. 165 – 187 and M. Duffy, *The Erotic World of Faery* (London: Hodder and Stoughton, 1972).

[14] Zipes, *When Dreams Came True*, pp. 125 – 126.

[15] Letter to Marchette and Joy Chute, 28th December, 1973. In Maxwell, op. cit., p. 272.

[16] Sylvia Townsend Warner, *The Portrait of a Tortoise* (London: Chatto and Windus, 1946).

[17] The two other examples of this genre I have found are Byron Rogers' biography of Ali Pasha, a tortoise captured from the Turks at Gallipoli and now living in a garden in Lowestoft - in his *An Audience with an Elephant* (London: Penguin Books, 2003) – and R. K. Bruce's *Timothy the Tortoise*, the life of a tortoise who lived at Powderham Castle in Devon for some 160 years (London: Orion, 2004).

[18] The comment on Stalin is made in the diary entry for 30th October 1961 (Harman, op. cit., p. 277), for Townsend Warner's view of Baroness Thatcher see letter to Ben Hellman, 29th January, 1976 in Maxwell, op. cit., p. 286.

CHAPTER 4

Sylvia Townsend Warner and the Politics of the English Pastoral 1925 – 1934

Mary Jacobs

What did 'the pastoral' mean to Sylvia Townsend Warner? Between 1925 and 1934 she published three books of poems: *The Espalier* (1925), *Time Importuned* (1928) and *Whether a Dove or Seagull*, the last jointly written and published with Valentine Ackland (1934); three novels: *Lolly Willowes* (1926), *Mr Fortune's Maggot* (1927) and *The True Heart* (1929); a single-volume extended narrative poem, *Opus 7* (1931), and various small-press collections of short stories, grouped together as *The Salutation* in 1932. Although remarkably various in content, style and setting, her writing in this period, whether set in the Chilterns, the Essex marshes, a Dorset valley, Polynesia or South America, shares a preoccupation with the lie of the land and the representation of its common people interacting with - or acted upon by - their masters and 'betters'. These are matters that have found expression in the pastoral mode for more than two millennia; Warner gives them a uniquely wry, graceful and subversive consideration. She looks back to the examples of Crabbe, Clare and Hardy, but also forward, formulating an approach in which class and gender aspects are subtly interrogated by means of stylistic and narrative experiment.

In this essay I shall use the literary paradigm of the pastoral to examine the emerging politics and changing aesthetics of Warner's engagement with 'the country'. In 1935 she and her partner Valentine Ackland joined the Communist

Party of Great Britain, but unlike many others on the Left they did not base their political activity in the city. Rather, they worked to form a 'Dorset Popular Front', active in the Dorset Peace Council, lending the Hammonds' *Village Labourer* and Engels' *The Condition of the Working Class in England* to their neighbours. By 1939 Warner saw moving to and living in the countryside as the essential step in her radicalisation[1]. However, her connection to the pastoral is by no means straightforward. I shall examine how her relationship with a literary form claimed as both conservative and radical, artificial and simple, serves to clarify her status as a writer variously identified as 'Georgian' and 'Modernist'.

During the inter-war period the countryside was the subject of huge ideological investment. Stanley Baldwin's assertion, 'To me, England is the country, and the country is England'[2], is part of a conservative nostalgic discourse which evokes an idealised pre-war English countryside as it justifies and romanticises post-war Empire and 'Dominion'. Rural writing was perceived to have 'a crucial role in keeping metropolitan, imperial Britain in touch with her roots'[3], testified in the popularity of Mary Webb's novels and the pastoral lyrics of the Georgian poets. Jan Marsh[4] has demonstrated how a middle-class love of the countryside and a fascination with rural 'lore', folk culture and peasant mentors had developed in Edwardian England. Building on the rhetoric of late-Victorian Christian Socialism and the thought of William Morris, this idealisation of both land and folk was a response to a decline in religious observance and to growth in the cities as agricultural labour was recruited into the factories. Ruralism between the wars drew on this inheritance, but added to it a nostalgia for an idealised, *pre-war,* paradisal English countryside. 'The country' was thus imbued with patriotism, spirituality and authenticity, attributes sharing a conservative sense of the importance of origins, continuity and tradition. However, a different inflection of the pastoral is evident in the romanticised espousal of vagabondage and the cult of 'the open road', where 'something that the ancients thought divine can be found, and felt there still'[5]. This exemplifies a strand of ruralism that implies resistance to the efficiencies of modernity: the familiar atavistic relish for the ancient, seen as synonymous with the divine, is here accompanied by a refusal to be confined. This nomadic and playful nuance of ruralism needs to be set alongside the sense of an ordered and productive landscape described above, as an additional aspect of the pastoral. For inter-war writers then, including Mary Webb, the Georgian poets and Sylvia Townsend Warner, 'the country' could suggest positive ascriptions for the fleeting and the feral along with the more familiar comforts of a rural community celebrating harvest home in the Shropshire cornfields.

However, that Victorian flight of labour to the city was the subject of a satirical note in J.B. Priestley's 1934 *English Journey*: 'You do not hurry out of Arcadia to work in a factory twelve hours a day for about eighteenpence'[6]. Priestley's implied critique of living conditions within the countryside that had been invoked as 'the real England' was shared by others. Warner's friend J.W. Robertson-Scott offered a searing account of contemporary rural poverty in *England's Green and Pleasant Land: the Truth Attempted*. Using the documentary approach later employed by Valentine Ackland in her 1936 *Country Conditions* - for which Warner worked out the statistics concerning the Milk Marketing Board - he notes the irony by which the hamlet, 'hovel-housed ... physically, mentally and morally impoverished', has nonetheless been ready to send its 'lads' to death in the Great War. Educated intervention among 'these submerged neighbours and brethren'[7] is, he decides, the moral imperative. Priestley and Robertson-Scott remind us of the other side of the pastoral idyll, as does Warner in her conclusion that 'the English pastoral was a grim and melancholy thing'[8]. In doing so they are, paradoxically, remaining constant to a longstanding aspect of the pastoral mode, its tension between mythical and naturalistic elements.

Critical accounts of the pastoral have wrestled with the form's difficulty of definition and with the ideological implications of its various manifestations from

Hesiod writing in the eighth century B.C. to the present-day eco-feminism of Ursula Le Guin (an enthusiast for Sylvia Townsend Warner, incidentally[9]). To trace Warner's use of the pastoral and her development of a style which I shall characterise as 'fantastic ruralism', I will use four features of the pastoral mode - the Golden Age and its implied return in the Georgic; the 'beautiful relation' between rich and poor; the pastoral turn; and the celebration of the 'humble thing' - to discuss the politics and aesthetics of their varying manifestations in Warner's writing between 1925 and 1934.

In the Golden Age, first known to western classical tradition through Hesiod, men lived like gods, ('without sorrow of heart, remote and free from toil and grief ... the fruitful earth unforced bore them fruit abundantly and without stint'), in contrast to a present 'when men never rest from labour and sorrow'[10]. 'The Golden Age is portrayed normally as a series of negations of the world produced by history ... shadowing the real world as an undisposable "other", the world of desire'[11]. However, this vision, later identified with Arcadia, has the potential to return, as described in the rapturous prophecy of Virgil's *Eclogue IV*, 'The Golden Age Returns', with radical implications, both aesthetically and politically. The pastoral's conflation of place (Arcadia) and time (the Golden Age) and its derivation from a classical notion of history as cyclic, offer hope as well as nostalgia: 'the notion of making time pause, even stop, or circle back to the beginning (stretching duration, in other words) is basic to the pastoral instinct for enclosure'[12]. The pastoral mode's experiments with duration and sequence have engendered some astonishing literary effects, including the reversal, cancellation or writing out of time itself. Such challenging narrative experiment is an enduring characteristic of Warner's aesthetic, most often associated with the landscape. Politically, the Golden Age becomes a radical exemplar: Warner's use of this aspect of the pastoral between the wars incorporates aspects of Virgil's later work, the *Georgics*. The *Georgics* contain practical advice on vine-pruning and bee-keeping: Nature is regarded in terms of necessary labour rather than harmonious idleness, and this is not a matter for post-lapsarian regret but for some celebration. The vision is that of an organic community characterised by free labour, an image later valued by the English Radical tradition and to which Warner alludes in her account of the political education that the countryside gave her.

The concept of the 'beautiful relation' comes from William Empson's *Some Versions of Pastoral*. His discussion of the pastoral - 'a puzzling form which looks proletarian but isn't' - emphasises the political from the outset, differentiating between fairy stories and ballads produced *by* and *for* the people but mostly not *about* them, and the pastoral which though *about* is not *by* or *for* them. He notes the pastoral's interaction between courtiers and shepherds as seeming to imply 'a beautiful relation between rich and poor'[13]. Whereas Empson identifies its conservative potential, the idea is echoed more sympathetically in Robertson-Scott's recommendations for working as a Tolstoyan missionary in the depressed hamlet, which Warner applauded, although she treated it ironically in her account of another missionary, Mr Timothy Fortune.

The pastoral turn is exemplified in the form's constitutionally interrogative nature, founded as it is on oppositional ironies. From the beginning, Arcadia has been 'other'. For some, the pastoral encourages a political analysis which should lead to change; for others, it underwrites the status quo by encouraging us to feel 'that we ought to accept the injustice of society as we do the inevitability of death'[14]. Whatever our conclusion, it is the pastoral turn that has prompted it: the representation of a simple and sequestered life is contrasted with an implied complex urban world; or the evocation of a rich and free past offers a counterpoint to a straitened and oppressed present. In addition to the pastoral's fruitful opposition with an unpastoral world, the form itself has its own 'other side of the landscape' in the anti-pastoral, in which the idyll of the literary convention is juxtaposed with the bitter reality of life on the land. Warner's description of the genesis of her 1931 *Opus 7* acknowledges her debt to that aspect of the pastoral turn: 'It was towards the end of this decade that I bethought me that it was about time to try to do for this date what Crabbe had done for his: write a truthful pastoral in the jog-trot English couplet'[15]. Writing a 'truthful pastoral' could mean letting the poor speak out about their troubles, but the representation in writing of those who do not write has always been problematic, as Empson's consideration of 'the humble thing' reveals.

For Empson, pastoral protagonists do not have to be shepherds or even farmers. *Some Versions of Pastoral* also considers childhood as a pastoral space and goes further in widening the potential pastoral category to an identification of pastoral as 'the humble thing, with mystical respect for poor men, fools and children', citing the old saying that 'the fool sees true' as having 'a touch of the pastoral'[16]. These concepts recall the world of Warner's 1929 *The True Heart*, whose chief protagonists are a poor girl and a holy fool in a Georgic setting. That novel tellingly links the positioning of those 'humble' people, othered by the powerful as primitive types, to the parallel assumptions and contradictions of the imperialist project. The discourses of cultural primitivism in the twentieth century include both derogation of the primitive as unregenerate beast and idealisation as pre-lapsarian man, 'such as live after the manner of the Golden Age', antithetical categories which Warner explores in her treatment of 'the humble thing'.

However, as we have noted, when Warner began to write poetry and fiction in the 1920s, 'the country' despite being the site of poverty, depopulation and exploitation was simultaneously being celebrated as the apotheosis of patriotism, spirituality and authenticity. As already suggested, the pastoral has been claimed by both radical and conservative traditions; while having the power to reassure or at least to promote an acceptance of 'inevitability', the pastoral turn has been equally able to facilitate social criticism as far back as Virgil's *Eclogue I*, 'The Dispossessed'. However, the question of whether or not the *representation* of radical rural content can be equally iconoclastic is more problematic, though particularly interesting in Warner's case in terms of her development of 'fantastic ruralism' from elements of the pastoral form and the popular rural writing of the period, to which I will now turn.

Commenting on the popularity of 'rural writing' between the wars, Anthea Trodd contrasts the appropriation of such material by Tory forces with the more subversive views of some women writers themselves. Whereas Stanley Baldwin's famous preface to Mary Webb's 1929 *Precious Bane* emphasised the nation's continuity with its rural past and Woman's special relationship with Nature, Webb herself stressed the tragically 'lost-and-forgotten lives' of working rural women, and the countryside as a 'secret treasurable resource for working people'[17]. Today, Webb is probably best known of the inter-war ruralist writers, partly through her satirical commentator Stella Gibbons' *Cold Comfort Farm*. Equally a target for Gibbons' satire was T. F. Powys, of great importance for Warner's writing in this period. Although located in the Dorset countryside to which he introduced Warner, his novels lack the biting satire of inter-war rural conditions that Warner brings to bear in *Opus 7*. Rather, Powys' largely malicious peasants grapple within a dark cosmogony, devoid of historical or social analysis. Despite their differences, the rural setting is vital to Webb, Powys, Gibbons and Warner for what are seen as its elemental qualities and their inter-relationship with the religious impulse. The relationship between the land and the people is depicted with varying emphases on sacred and social factors, revealing a range of ideological positions.

The shifts within Warner's fusing of the land with a sense of the numinous and the fleeting relationship of that sense to Christianity in this early period are evident in 'Peeping Tom' from *The Espalier*[18]; the paean to Spring and the contrapuntal reproach to Nature in *Opus 7*[19]; and the invocation of an earth-goddess in the Grannie Moxon poem 'Wintry is this April' from *Whether a Dove or Seagull*[20]. Each demonstrates aspects of the elements contributing to Warner's adaptation of the pastoral and rural writing into fantastic ruralism.

'Peeping Tom', dedicated to Powys and developed from a Holy Fool character in his 1923 novella *The Left Leg*, initially shows a politicised response to rural poverty: landless Tom longs, like John Clare, for a half-acre 'To be my land/And mine alone'. Granted his wish, Tom struggles fruitlessly against the elements until he receives a vision: 'Nature, hidden under her dark veils of Time and Space and Causation' invites him to learn her secret. The secret revealed by the spirit of place in *Lolly Willowes* is Laura's vocation as a witch, a wise woman with a fund of folk knowledge; in the Powysian 'Peeping Tom', it is the land's beauty rather than its usefulness. Tom's efforts at 'resolution and independence' are abandoned as he becomes a contemplative nature mystic. The poem ends with its narrator visiting Tom's patch but failing to recognise him in 'one old man/Scarcely more human' than the gulls, who stares intently at a weed, 'and then/Throwing it down,/Limped on again'. This final haunting image is an early example of a trope in Warner's work of the enduring poor man, a type who persists across time and space, representing the common folk. The idea, not unrelated to primitivist assumptions about those who live outside time and history, and current in those aspects of popular rural writing that are satirised by Stella Gibbons, owes something more to the romantic socialism of Edward Thomas' 'Lob'. In Thomas' poem rural knowledge, craft and regional specificities are stressed; the tramp who helps Sukey in *The True Heart* is more Lob-like than Peeping Tom, having a history which demonstrates the roots of poverty in specific social circumstances. 'Lob' ends with an image remarkably similar to the close of 'Peeping Tom': the narrator sees 'one glimpse of his back' as the enduring man continues on his wandering way. Whereas Thomas' rural-romantic socialism is evident in Lob's claim for ramblers' rights to the common ground – 'Nobody can't stop 'ee. It's/A footpath, right enough' – the politics of Warner's poem move away from protest at rural dispossession to nature mysticism. But it is the disquieting final image of poverty and discontent that lingers. 'Nature' in 'Peeping Tom' is feminised, remote and beautifully useless, but not the subject of reproach for these non-Georgic qualities. Rather, this representation of Nature illustrates that resistant aspect of early twentieth-century ruralism noted earlier, its distaste for the social utility of the modernising project: 'the cult of nature celebrated forms of redundancy, eccentricity and sheer uselessness'[21]. The impulse is attractive to a range of political positions; in Warner's case, even as early as 'Peeping Tom', she demonstrates unease with the aestheticising of rural poverty, leaving her reader troubled, gazing after the limping, ragged man.

In *Opus 7* the rapturous and elegiac paean to Spring (ll. 403 – 459) is immediately succeeded by an antithetical account of 'Nature'(ll.460 – 495). Such juxtaposition is typical of the approach of this extended narrative poem which establishes a technique of jarring but productive disorientation from its first few lines. Warner contrasts a specific post-war historical setting with an archaic vocabulary which is further out of kilter both with its formal debt to Clare and Crabbe and additionally in its references to phenomena specific to the time of its composition (1929-30). The paean to Spring, 'most dear,/most dolorous virgin-mother of the year' is a rare passage of autobiographical first-person narration in which the poet reflects on Spring as a symbol for renaissance in both art and life. She refers to its signs in America where she'd been a guest critic on the *New York Herald Tribune* in 1929 – 'myself watching a redskin river flow/eastward to the Atlantic' – and, in a Metaphysical trope, employs it as a self-referential image of artistic renewal followed by necessary disillusion. The account of Nature which then follows juxtaposes town and country in traditional pastoral/anti-pastoral style: whereas a glimpse of her 'green kerchief' delights her devotees in town, in the country the goddess 'a more real tribute entertains', as Warner describes the struggles of shepherds, hoers and smallholders against the whims of Nature, now figured as a fickle 'immortal doxy'. Dependent on her caprice is the impoverished Rebecca Random who determinedly grows flowers to buy gin, becoming a 'sorceress', 'priestess' and 'mystic' in her drinking rites. In *Opus 7* then, Warner combines political analysis of inter-war rural poverty with attitudes to nature varying from the mystical to the satirical, but significantly couples these with a Modernist self-conscious commentary on artistic production and with elaboration of the concept of the rural witch-woman's struggle for independence, self-expression and social power.

'Wintry is this April', about 'Grannie' Moxon, a villager in East Chaldon, emphasises the difficulty and duration of her labour and invests her with a trans-historical significance as 'Gardener long-lineaged'. This not only twins her as 'wise woman' with the trope of the 'enduring man' already mentioned, but also scandalously incorporates a particular old Dorset woman into the Judaeo-Christian mythology of Eden. Grannie is thus simultaneously symbolic and affectionately particularised. Having used Christian references transgressively – 'And with Christ aloft on cross and combed out our sin/Potatoes in' – the poem moves towards an ecstatic nature vision: 'Some brief and lovely phrase in a language unknown:/A chance-cast net as idly trawled over flesh/As the bright mesh/Of birdsong'. Warner figures this ecstasy in relation to the female body and the landscape. The poem concludes with an invocation to this vision, embodied as a pagan nature goddess, to beatify her poor servant, the implication being that the patriarch Jehovah won't. Mother-goddess and old working woman seem to merge as Grannie is celebrated, rewarded and transfigured in a mystical finale both theological and agricultural, which, valorising the maternal body, avoids the satire of *Opus 7* entirely: 'Not she, not she, but earth's very spirit/Rose to inherit/Light everlasting, the manifested coronal/Of long darkness, of long-ploughed patience/Long acquiescence/Of the nourishing breast, of the receiving lap'.

Investing nature, the land and its people with near-mystical significance in this way was characteristic of much 'stock' ruralism of the period, exemplified in Powys and Webb, satirised in Gibbons and used in both ways by Warner. In *The True Heart* there are elements which border on the primitivism of Webb but like Gibbons veer towards comedy (though Sukey, the 'true heart' herself, is usually distanced from such satirical treatment). 'The old man never speaks, and no more don't his sons. Young Eric's a ninny. As for Zeph, he's Peculiar...'[22] remarks Prue: we feel ourselves to be at Cold Comfort. However, the passage in which Sukey is required to kill a cockerel by 'sticking' it (the pig-killing episode from *Jude the Obscure* is evoked) is transformed from the conventionalised rural violence of Powys and parts of Webb into a far more subtle psychological exploration appropriately expressed in an unorthodox narration in which time is suspended. Sukey's long internal monologue 'I am like a ghost ... I am like a dream...'(p.68) explores her present disorientation and resentment at Eric's inability to uphold a stereotypical gender role, while presaging the birth of her new subjectivity and politicisation in the subsequent part of the novel. Here we have moved far from the decorum of the later Georgians' country matters: Modernist elements – the representation of a fractured consciousness – are linked to gender and class politics, emerging from a transformative inter-relationship with popular ruralism. Similarly Warner's remarkable and little-known novella of this period, 'Elinor Barley' (collected in *The Salutation* of 1932)[23], enhances and complicates the spare dimensions of its folk-song starting-point, 'The Brisk Young Widow'. Extraordinarily subtle in its detailed study of abjection, surprisingly anticipative of aspects of feminist theory in its use of the mirror to explore the split self, Modernist in its self-conscious commentary on its own narrative which must end with its narrator's execution for her husband's murder, this text, while making use of pastoral and Georgic elements, transforms the standard properties of ruralism. Here is a ballad which deeply unsettles the decorous Georgian use of folk song and - *pace* Empson - is *about* the people. By means of its formal innovation as well as its gendered analysis it indicates the development of Warner's fantastic ruralism.

I shall now turn to Warner's use of the Golden Age as modified by the Georgic vision of the English Radical tradition. In the post-lapsarian world of Christian mythology, two possibilities inform the pastoral's depiction of the people on the land: a starveling peasant's pinched and oppressed existence under feudalism, or a Georgic-inflected return to a modified Golden Age in an organic community characterised by free labour. This contrast has been of vital importance for the English Radical tradition to which Warner alludes, citing the Hammonds' *The Village Labourer, Piers Plowman,* Cobbett's *Rural Rides,* Crabbe, Clare, Bunyan, Burns and Robertson-Scott[24]. The social relations implied within the organic community, recalling Langland's 'fair field full of folk ... Of all manner of men', while harmonious, depend upon recognition by its leaders of their responsibilities; equally important is the celebration of what Empson called 'a pastoral feeling about the dignity of labour'. Such rural labour is configured as skilled craft (recalling William Morris' 1885 *Useful Work versus Useless Toil*) rather than embodying the repressive notion of work as necessary for the moral discipline of the poor. This vision (to use Langland's term) of social relations, labour and the land has been called 'Merry England', a term likely today to suggest a nostalgic conservatism. But this is rather the Merry England of Edward Thomas' 'The Manor Farm'. This poem which itself exemplifies the conflation of past time and pastoral place describes the awakening of a frozen farm landscape to the arrival of Spring in terms that suggest the potential for a corresponding social awakening to a revived Golden Age:

> But 'twas not Winter –
> Rather a season of bliss unchangeable
> Awakened from farm and church where it had lain
> Safe under tile and thatch for ages since
> This England, Old already, was called Merry. [25]

How then are the Golden Age and its modified return in the Georgic vision represented in Warner's works from this period, and with what political and aesthetic implications? It is the *lack* of a Georgic vision that is delineated in the sharply particularised poverty of the village Love Green in *Opus 7*: Rebecca Random, while a priestess and witch woman like Laura Willowes is, unlike her, grindingly poor; Love Green, unlike Great Mop, is pinchpenny and suspicious.

Lolly Willowes[26] contains elements of a Georgic vision in its references to brewing and farming, subtly coloured by the novel's gender politics and fantastic qualities. Although religion of a charitable kind generally supports the economy of any village represented in the Georgic mode, its foremother, magic, is singularly lacking. However, the vision which ends Lolly's constrained London life is a magical as well as a Georgic one: she imagines the 'lean wiry old woman' who grows fruit and flowers, 'as though she were a tree herself, growing out of the long grass, with arms stretched up like branches' (83). It is in the wild woods rather than the farmland that the spirit of the place and Satan reside; indeed when Titus' appearance in the village compromises Laura's vocation and 'the spirit of the place withdrew itself further from her', Great Mop threatens to become merely 'a pastoral landscape where an aunt walked with her nephew' (161). 'Pastoral' here then seems to stand against magic and 'the wild zone', signifying a settled landscape under masculine authority as Laura imagines Titus' possession of the land: 'He could walk in the greenest meadow and have dominion over it like a bull' (155). Nonetheless there are Georgic elements in the depictions of individuals engaged in rural work - Mr Saunter's poultry-keeping, Laura's knowledge of herbs - which tellingly is figured here as craft rather than labour. However, although the villagers are an organic community, Satan rather than a charitable priest of the Georgic tradition (Goldsmith's and Clare's 'good old vicar') is their spiritual exemplar; the text's fantastic elements serve to valorise an alternative world rather than a politically reformed one.

Warner's Georgic vision finds its most unambiguous expression in the idyllic conclusion of *The True Heart* when Sukey's fidelity and industry find their reward with the 'simple' Eric Seaborn in 'a country life ... a settled life' (287). Warner specifically acknowledges Virgil's *Georgics* in the bee-keeping which will become Eric's peaceful occupation, and the politics of the Georgic vision are suggested in Mr Warburton's meditation on bees' social organisation: 'For bees are in an especial manner dear to Jove, who in gratitude for that first sweetness taught them a policy and ordered living by which above all beasts and even man they exemplify majestic law: Virgil says so...' (291). However, *The True Heart* closes with a sense of the limitations as well as the satisfactions of the Georgic life. Sukey, labouring to give birth to her daughter Joy, is visited with a sense of loss: the clarity of her 'maiden' self is departing as Mrs Lucy the midwife replaces the sphinx, '[w]ild, proud, mournful and steadfast ... inscrutably sisterly' (258) who has been her totem. The sphinx, along with much else in this novel, belongs to a symbolic economy which, like the shifting and liminal marsh landscape in which it is largely set, eludes containment by the fruitfulness and order of the Georgic vision. Those aspects of the text's representation of the rural imply a different politics in which gendered analysis and narrative experiment produce a fantastic ruralism at odds with a Georgic aesthetic.

Warner's investigation of the pastoral mode and its Georgic aspect was of course itself the product of how the form was understood and employed in the 1920s and early 1930s and therefore implicated in the politics of the 'beautiful relation': her investment in Robertson-Scott's model of educated intervention is evident in her account of visits to his 'Simple Life' community at Idbury. (It is less attractively shown in her patronising portrait in 'Love Green' of Jimmy, the 'enlightened man' of the village 'who enjoys as he said himself, "books of any nature, poetical, historical, historilolical, or Scriptural" '[27] and to whom she lends her copy of Lecky's *History of European Morals* (p.220). A comic primitivism seems to be at play here; the mocking treatment of the risible autodidact cannot be denied.) Just as the full title of Phillip Gibbs' 1935 *England Speaks*, published to celebrate George V's Silver Jubilee, ran: *Being Talks with Roadsweepers, Barbers, Statesmen, Lords and Ladies, Beggars, Farming Folk, Actors, Artists, Literary Gentlemen, Tramps, Down-and-outs, Miners, Steelworkers, Blacksmiths, The-Man-in-the-Street, Highbrows, Lowbrows and all manner of folk of humble and exalted rank. With a panorama of the English scene in this year of grace, 1935*[28], so Warner's delineation of the 'workaday democracy' shared by women and working class writers 'who have got into literature by the pantry window'[29] refes to their 'ease and appreciativeness in low company' and 'willing ear for the native tongue, for turns of phrase used by carpenters, gardeners, sailors, milliners, tinkers, old nurses, and that oldest nurse of all, ballad and folklore' (p. 272). The romantic socialism of such positions is ironically open to the old radical charge against the pastoral: that it proposes an unhistorical relationship between the ruling class and the workers on the land, obscuring the reality of socio-economic organisation. The semi-comic hyperbole of both Gibbs' and Warner's syntax employs the aesthetic of an underlying Bakhtinian carnivalesque, playfully subverting an urban cultural hegemony while simultaneously dependent on the 'beautiful relation' to underpin their ideological positions.

Treatment of the 'beautiful relation' in *The True Heart* is interestingly double-edged. On her quest to see Queen Victoria, Sukey arrives at dawn in Covent Garden Market where porters, costers and flower-women are already at work: 'Besides these workaday folk Sukey saw with bewilderment a quantity of gentry, all youthful, grand and gay, and dressed as though for a ball. In a proper gentry manner they did not appear to be doing anything except enjoy themselves ... seeming perfectly at home' (236). From this milieu, accompanied by an improbable blue dog, emerges Lord Constantine Melhuish whose sister, a Lady-in Waiting, will providentially take Sukey to the Queen. Constantine approves Sukey's vision of a England united 'under the dome' of the matriarch; he praises her feral qualities in terms recalling the idealising primitivist aesthetic that links Woman and Nature: 'she is like ... any small feather the wind blows along the ground ... so intent on being a feather, so - ...Oh fairies, Ruskin, anything you like' (247). So far, so cosy then: this is the world in which Phillip Gibbs' 'folk of humble and exalted rank' would later mingle under a benevolent George V. It is also the point at which David Garnett lost faith with *The True Heart*: '[a]fter her arrival in London I don't like it at all ... you invite the reader to feel superior to your heroine ... she's only an aunt sally and a half-wit ... I see you playing with hellfire the moment that dog arrives in Covent Garden'[30]. But Covent Garden's fantastical panorama is not the novel's only example of class relations and Sukey is no half-wit. Earlier in the novel, her supplication to the Lady Patroness Mrs Seaborn, whose 'idiot' son she loves and whose child she believes she is carrying, has been rewarded by a smashing blow across her mouth from that grand lady. Now, preparing to see the Queen, Sukey knows she cannot share the nature of her plan even with these benevolent aristocrats: she is well aware of the power of the class system and the patriarchal state to punish the poor: 'people could act their disapproval, could clash those iron gates in her face, bid those fixed bayonets level their steel glance at her, send a policeman to take her to prison, a warder to carry Eric to the madhouse …they disapprove when a servant girl marries a gentleman …' (250). The kindly Lady Emily, kitting her out for the interview with the Queen, pointedly provides Sukey with new *servant's* garments: 'trimmings were for the glorious, the guarded, the unbeseeching, who kissed the Queen's hand and went away to the ball. She was here upon a workaday errand …'(259). The novel's Georgic plot resolution in fact depends upon the upper-classes *requiring* Sukey to marry Eric to preserve the family's respectability. Class and gender aspects of a politicised analysis thus intersect with the familiar oppositions of the pastoral impulse and are combined with a knowing use of fantasy.

Gender also tends to subvert those elements of the 'beautiful relation' that are present in *Lolly Willowes*. Laura's comfortable equality with her landlady Mrs Leak in Great Mop is interrupted by the arrival of her cousin Titus: 'in conjunction they became gentry' (185). It is Titus who discovers a superficial cultured 'rusticity' in the village which had passed Laura by entirely: 'He congratulated Laura upon having discovered so unspoilt an example of the village community' (159). In fact this 'community' bears the same relation to Great Mop's real secrets as the false Satan - 'an impostor, a charlatan, a dummy' - bears to the 'real Satan', the Loving Huntsman who may always be found in the wood

(207). The falsely bucolic 'village community' into which Titus is welcomed typifies the 'beautiful relation' and satirises a Simple Life drained of political engagement:

> He passed from the bar-parlour of the Lamb and Flag to the rustic woodwork of the rector's lawn. He subscribed to the bowling-green fund, he joined the cricket club, he engaged himself to give readings at the Institute during the winter evenings. He was invited to become a bell-ringer, and to read the lessons. He burgeoned with projects for Co-operative Blue Beverens, morris-dancing and performing Coriolanus with the Ancient Foresters, getting Henry Wappenshaw to come down and paint a village sign, inviting Pandora Williams and her rebeck for the Barleighs Flower Show (159).

Sukey knows how the power of policeman and asylum warder underlies the 'beautiful relation' that disguised the reality of class relations and eugenics; for Laura, patriarchy has the power to cancel out her economic and class privilege: 'Custom, public opinion, law, church and state – all would have ... sent her back to bondage' (220).

What can be set against such power seems and is humble: it is 'the humble thing', that subversive notion of the countryside as 'a secret treasurable resource for working people' whose politics and aesthetics help to constitute Warner's 'fantastic ruralism'. Consider Lolly, reborn as Laura Willowes in Great Mop: 'She was changed, and knew it. She was humbler, and more simple' (149). Empson's formulation of the pastoral as 'the humble thing, with mystical respect for poor men, fools and children'[31] does not refer to women, though he may have felt that they were embraced within his categories. But it is women in Warner's pastoral writings who are the principal guardians and practitioners of an arcane knowledge about a rural past living on secretly under the present. It has the power through folk magic, rather than Georgic religion, to transform the lives of the dispossessed. Warner's depiction of such power is not sentimental; its avatar Mrs Disbrowe, 'Godmother', is a pub landlady who knows 'The True Secret of

England's Greatness' and is revealed in *The True Heart* as the real Queen of England, rather than Victoria R.I. Warner links her to a specific use of the word 'good' which signals the persisting power of the old ways. 'Goody' was, like 'Grannie', an honorific title for an old country woman; in *The True Heart* the persistence of folk wisdom which will outlast modernity is invoked through objects associated with Mrs Disbrowe which are indeed 'the humble thing': 'having all about her, just as the linen-cupboard, the copper-kettle and the tea-caddy had, the air of being certain to last for a long time ... the air of being Good' (215). When Mrs Disbrowe describes herself as 'old-fashioned', the term signals religious power. 'Godmother ... don't hold with the clergy' (222); she exemplifies a folk magic that precedes and will outlast Anglicanism, an idea depicted without irony or sentiment in Sukey's dream-vision of her visit to London under Godmother's protection: 'Mrs Disbrowe standing where she had left her, standing patient and superb as she had stood in the pasture. Around her the houses of London had dwindled so that they rose no higher than her knees and grass was growing from the pavement' (220—21). Here the pastoral, manifest as fantastic ruralism, has overpowered town, church, monarchy, patriarchy and modernity itself.

Such subversive and demotic imaging of power nevertheless has roots in a primitivist discourse which locates the categories of 'Woman' and 'Nature', like 'natives', as outside time and history. The notion of a secret, unwritten lore can bear the same confining symbolic freight as 'prehistory' in figuring the relations between woman, folk and land. The valorisation of craft objects from a time preceding mass production may betray a conservative anxiety underlying a carnivalesque celebration of folk culture, and can be expressed as regulatory class relations. (Such an element is evident in 'Love Green' where the contemporary villagers' fondness for 'trumpery' from Woolworth's is regretfully contrasted with the objects appreciated by 'a previous generation ... something solid – a marble-topped washstand or a set of grand fire-irons' (224). Here, 'popular' is urban and meretricious, while 'folk' is rural and 'good'.) The patriotic Tory potential within such a discourse of an ancient folk culture was harnessed in Stanley Baldwin's *On England* (contemporaneous with *Lolly Willowes*), leading to a nationalist analysis. Referring to 'that wood smoke that our ancestors, tens of thousands of years ago, must have caught on the air ... when they were still nomads', Baldwin explains that 'These things strike down into the very depths of our nature, and touch chords that go back to the beginning of time and the human race'.[32]

Warner's textual negotiations with folk culture, prehistory and magic generally avoid the conservative and patriotic implications of such ascriptions. As we have seen, the politics of her 'humble thing' are complicated by anti-clericalism and her radical treatment of gender and class; the aesthetics of its presentation are similarly enhanced by a Modernist awareness of myth and an engagement with ethnography, together with dazzlingly adroit narrative time-shifts. The presence of Polynesia in *Mr Fortune's Maggot* and classical paganism in *The True Heart* militate against appropriation of Warner's pastoral world by little-Englandism or by preoccupations with blood and soil. The narrative framework of *The True Heart*, while working with the properties of folk-tale, ballad and fairy story, derives from the classical myth of Eros and Psyche and, as we have seen, employs Virgilian references to promote a Georgic vision. Within the overall economy of the novel, classical and folk cultures are accorded equal value. In *Mr Fortune's Maggot*, the old wise woman Hina's Polynesian 'legends and fairy-tales' prove to be 'almost word for word the stories of the Old Testament' (152). The politics of this range of cultural references militate against the exclusions of 'othering': cultural phenomena are merely various rather than Other. But this is not to say that the ultimate effect is one of simple equanimity: aesthetically these features draw attention to the provisional and fabricated nature of their own narratives, unsettling any over-easy acceptance of the diegesis as an authorised version. Often they exemplify the feral and erotic 'wild zone', as when

Bacchus arrives in Rebecca Random's Love Green cottage with full retinue, including leopards: 'How soft his leopards pad your kitchen floor!-/and with their thick tails buffet you, and thresh/sharp waves of joy along your drowsy flesh'[33]. The margins of space and place are equally fertile sources for Warner's explorations of social constraints. For Lolly Willowes, 'the clue to the secret country of her mind' (135) has always seemed about to reveal itself within physically liminal contexts which rouse 'a kind of ungodly hallowedness': 'her mind walked by lonely sea-bords, in marshes and fens, or came at nightfall to the edge of a wood' (76, 77). Significantly, these 'edges' of the landscape typify those who, like the spinster, are 'of the margins': Lolly's restless London wanderings have taken her to the East End, to the lane beside the Bayswater Synagogue, and to the Jews' Burying Ground. Relocated to Great Mop, aware of the politics of her spinsterhood, Laura comes to equate her position with that of an African American slave (149, 163); her witch's familiar, the Devil's kitten Vinegar, is also a starveling on the edges, 'sent out too young into the world, like a slavey from an Institution' (171-72), an account that exactly describes her next heroine, Sukey Bond. In that novel too, apparently settled systems of social organisation and control will be called into question, just as the shifting and magical attributes of its marsh landscape both disorientate and delight Sukey: 'It was dream-like indeed that she should be washing clothes and baking bread where once the fishes swam … small wonder that she felt astray from her proper self' (21).

Warner's transhistorical figures of the wise woman and the enduring man remain outsiders. Rather than becoming essentialist, or as Baldwin puts it, 'the things that make England', they are marginalised, deliberately equated, as we have seen, with those literally enslaved under Empire or with those who have been rendered 'like a slavey from an Institution', 'othered' by the constraints of hierarchical class or gender systems. They do not connect Warner's readers with their mythical prehistoric past so much as unsettle our relationship to the historical present. Warner's pastoral landscape is thus perpetually eroded by a sense of the liminal: whether the boundaries depicted in her writing seek to confine marshland, narrative time, class or gender, they are continually shifting and being remade.

University of Plymouth

Notes

[1] 'The Way by Which I Have Come', *The Countryman* July 1939 pp. 472 - 486

[2] *On England*, 1926, in Judy Giles and Tim Middleton, *Writing Englishness 1900 – 1950* London: Routledge 1995, p.101

[3] Anthea Trodd, *Women's Writing in English: Britain 1900 -1945* London: Longman 1998, p.104

[4] Jan Marsh, *Back to the Land: the Pastoral Impulse in Victorian England 1880-1914* London: Quartet Books, 1988

[5] Richard Jefferies, *The Amateur Poacher*, 1879, quoted in Jan Marsh, (1988), p. 34.

[6] Giles and Middleton 1995, p.105

[7] J. W. Robertson-Scott, *England's Green and Pleasant Land: the Truth Attempted*, Harmondsworth: Penguin, 1925, pp. 157, 158

[8] Warner 1939, p.478

[9] See, for example, Ursula Le Guin, 'Brief Encounter: Recollections of Sylvia Townsend Warner' in The Sylvia Townsend Warner Society Newsletter no. 9, Summer 2004

[10] Quoted by Lerner in Brian Loughrey (ed.) *The Pastoral Mode*, London: Methuen, 1984, p. 145

[11] Peter Weston, 'The Noble Primitive as Bourgeois Subject' in Loughrey 1984, p.173

[12] Andrew V. Ettin, *Literature and the Pastoral*, New Haven: Yale University Press 1984, p.142

[13] William Empson, (1935)*Some Versions of Pastoral*, London: Hogarth Press 1986, pp. 6, 11

[14] Empson 1986, p. 4

[15] Warner 1939, p.480

[16] Empson 1986, pp.21, 10

[17] Trodd 1998, p.108

[18] Warner, *The Espalier*, New York: The Dial Press 1925, pp. 92 – 103

[19] Warner, *Opus 7* in *Collected Poems*, Manchester: Carcanet New Press Ltd., 1982, lines 403 – 495)

[20] Sylvia Townsend Warner and Valentine Ackland, *Whether a Dove or Seagull*, London: Chatto and Windus 1934, pp. 20 – 26

[21] William Greenslade, '"Pan" and the Open Road: Critical Paganism in R.L.Stevenson, K.Grahame, E.Thomas and E.M.Forster' in Lynne Hapgood and Nancy L.Paxton (eds.), *Outside Modernism: In Pursuit of the English Novel 1900 – 1930*, Basingstoke: Macmillan, 2000, p.145.

[22] Warner, *The True Heart*, London: Virago 1978, p. 17

[23] Warner, *The Salutation*, Horam, East Sussex: The Tartarus Press, 2000

[24] Warner 1939 p. 478; and 'Women as Writers', 1959 lecture repr. in *Collected Poems*, pp.265 - 274.

[25] Edward Thomas, *Collected Poems*, London: Faber & Faber 1974, p. 25

[26] Warner, *Lolly Willowes* London: The Women's Press Ltd., 1978

[27] Warner, 'Love Green' in *The Nineteenth Century and After* August 1932 pp. 220 – 226

[28] Phillip Gibbs in Giles and Middleton, p.33

[29] Warner, 'Women as Writers', 1959 lecture reprinted in *Collected Poems* pp. 265 – 274

[30] Richard Garnett (ed.) *Sylvia and David: the Townsend Warner/Garnett Letters* London: Sinclair-Stevenson, 1994, p.45

[31] Empson 1986 p.21

[32] Stanley Baldwin in Giles and Middleton 1995 pp. 101-102

[33] Sylvia Townsend Warner, 'Opus 7' in *Collected Poems* (1982), p.217, ll.940 -943.

CHAPTER 5

A Counter-Reading to Conquest: "Primitivism" and Utopian Longing in Sylvia Townsend Warner's *Mr. Fortune's Maggot*

Emily M. Hinnov

Later, Sylvia Townsend Warner remembered finishing her novel *Mr. Fortune's Maggot* (1927) "in a state of semi-hallucination…then impulsively writing the envoy, with a feeling of compunction, almost guilt, towards this guiltless man I had created in such a fix" (qtd. in Harman 69). Indeed, she commented, "I love [Fortune] with a dreadful uneasy love which in itself denotes him a cripple" (70). Warner returned to the Timothy Fortune who seems to haunt her psyche in her novella *The Salutation* (1930), a sequel to *Mr. Fortune's Maggot* recently published for the first time. In her attendant comments, she expresses her dissatisfaction with the portrayal of Fortune, for whom she feels continual sympathy: "I wrote it out of my heart as an *amende* to poor Timothy…to show that I did not forget him" (124). Her need to write this "envoy" and the way in which she expresses sympathy for her character, suggests that Warner wrote her novel with a mixture of pity and derision for the typical English gentleman seeking to indoctrinate the "primitive Other" with the empire of religion. I find her attitude simultaneously problematic and fruitful.

Primitivism, as the inextricable symbiosis of black and white culture that calls upon racialist stereotypes, has been well-established as integral to the development of modernist aesthetics.[1] Yet Warner's ambivalent attitude resists the model of history that says white Europeans must continue doing what they have always done in inhabiting the space between self and other, even if only for ephemeral moments. Her uncertainty about her protagonist, complicated by my own uneasiness about her inevitable use of primitivism to suggest socio-political change, reveals a productive rift. I invite my collaborative reader to enter into this "third space," this threshold between empathy and distance, in order to uncover the potentially radical interplay between "primitivism" and utopian longing in Warner's novel.[2]

In this essay, I identify, describe and analyze textual moments of utopian unity, which I term "choran moments," created by Sylvia Townsend Warner in *Mr. Fortune's Maggot*. I argue that the choran moment, which reveals modern artists' treatment of the encounter between self and other, is typical of art in the interwar period. In using this term I do not mean to evoke the conventionally read "epiphanic moment" as focused on the solipsistic individual. Rather, the choran moment is a modernist aesthetic literary device resulting from correlation and wholeness between characters. My term draws upon Julia Kristeva's concept of "the semiotic chora," a prelinguistic state of consciousness experienced in infancy that suggests connection with the maternal body and therefore an integrated understanding of self. Expanding upon Kristeva's work, I argue that the longing to return to this moment allows modernist characters to rediscover a wholeness of self—the first step toward finding intersubjectivity and, finally, interconnective community.[3] Modernist woman author Sylvia Townsend Warner appropriates primitivism in her satirical, anti-imperialist novel *Mr. Fortune's Maggot* in order to create moments of prelinguistic unity, suggesting that we might actually be able to erase social borders between self and other.

In her novel's title, Warner intends the definition of maggot as a whimsical or perverse fancy. As *Mr. Fortune's Maggot* begins, the Reverend Timothy Fortune, ex-clerk of Lloyds Bank in London, has spent ten years as a South Seas Island missionary when a "maggot" impels him to embark on what he describes as "a sort of pious escapade"—an assignment to the even more remote island of Fanua, where a white man is a rarity. Mr. Fortune, a self-proclaimed good and humble man, wishes to bring the joys of Christianity to the innocent "heathen." But in his three years on Fanua he makes only one convert, the boy Lueli. The love between them produces in Fortune a shattering change in heart, and he decides to leave Fanua in the midst of a distant but impending world war.

Warner's novel rewrites notions of racist ideology by employing choran moments and interconnectivity to undercut the hegemony of empire. Former imperialist missionary Fortune's time on the island of Fanua and friendship with its initially most promising inhabitant, the young man Lueli, become a catalyst for both personal and collective renewal rather than exploitation. Their friendship can be viewed as the convergence of differences between self and other in light of Mary Louise Pratt's "contact zone." From this contact, a counter-narrative to conquest emerges. By his departure, the missionary has become the converted, and his new understanding suggests that Fortune may carry a reverse, anti-imperial message back to the old world (even in the midst of world war).

Mr. Fortune appears on the South Pacific island of Fanua as a typical English imperialist missionary man.[4] Fortune is quick to order his new environment, but he approaches this adventure as an excited, over-sexed adolescent might embrace the sensual abandon his new identity soon provides: "There seemed to be no end to the marvels and delights of his island, and he was thrilled as though he had been let loose into the world for the first time" (12). He is determined to live like "the natives" while simultaneously upholding his religious devotion and keeping his supposed superior morality intact. Gay Wachman argues convincingly that Warner's "apparently idyllic representation of oceanic sexuality...most explicitly draws upon (and satirizes) the utopian evolutionist sexology" of Edward Carpenter, the nineteenth-century sexologist who declared the superiority of "the intermediate sex" (70). Carpenter states that those more primitive people would "lead humankind toward a more spiritual, natural life in which the divisions of sex and gender would be transcended" (qtd. in Wachman 66). At the very least, Fortune embraces the opportunity to "go native" soon after he arrives on the island.

The natural life afforded by Fanua (its name ripe with both flora and fauna) seems, at first, to lead Fortune toward Carpenter's notion of sublime androgyny. Fortune extols the childlike simplicity of the island's beauty—"this gay landscape which might have been coloured out of a child's paint-box" (16). Yet Warner's narrator quickly contradicts Fortune's first response to the island's indigenous beauty. While Fortune initially primitivizes the seemingly pure landscape, apparently he is not able to comprehend its true beauty. He closes his eyes in a reverie of prayer and the narrator ironically comments: "from the expression on his face one would have said that he was all the more aware of the beauty around him for having his eyes shut, for he seemed like one in an ecstasy and his clasped hands trembled as though they had hold of a joy too great for him" (17-18). While "gazing with wonder and admiration" (18) at what he perceives as the Lord's handiwork, Fortune comes upon Lueli, "his first convert," whom he instantly renames "Theodore, which means the gift of God" (19). In one prolonged gaze over the countryside (and in the reverie of his inner vision), the Reverend Timothy Fortune has countenanced the power and beauty of nature laid bare solely for his personal, passionate benefit and established his authority by naming and thereby lay claim to the island's people, who are, from his perspective, also given to him by the Almighty God.[5]

Warner allows Fortune a series of similar moments of repose in the idyllic space he has come to encounter, cultivate and claim for his own, but she also presents her character as unstable and even comic. Fortune is clearly characterized as a masculine, colonialist missionary who becomes enraptured at the idea of providing tutelage for his only convert, the kind and docile young man, Lueli. Yet, like a fastidious housewife, he tidies his surroundings into a feminized domestic space—while simultaneously struggling against his oscillating desires for Lueli. Throughout their tumultuous relationship, as one critic puts it, "Timothy [Fortune] behaves more like a spurned lover than a wrathful saver of souls" (Rigby 228). Nigel Rigby argues that it is actually Lueli who performs this desire "to break down the reductive and destructive binaries through which European civilization constructed itself" in the text, that in his "tolerant feminine qualities, [he is more] receptive to difference" than Fortune (239-40). However, Warner's comic reversal also reconnects this Englishman with his own untainted nature through convergence with what he believes is a more authentic place. Her political point is that what turns out to be Fortune's self-conversion is only made available through his imperialist missionary work. Ultimately then, Warner is more radical than Rigby suggests because she posits the possibility that even the most stilted, sexually repressed, fanatically religious, British elitist can experience personal transformation, and that even when fraught with Fortune's perception of Fanua as archaic in the first place.

Furthermore, it is abundantly evident that Fortune will not succeed in his efforts to lay claim to the island or its inhabitants. Warner's decision to set the novel in a place yet to be tainted with colonialism demonstrates her desire to tell a different, perhaps anti-colonial, story. Moreover, the interaction between Lueli and Fortune reveals a healthy measure of the kind of sympathy (from both sides) necessary for revolutionizing relationships between otherwise would-be imperialists and the "natives" they seek to control. Fortune's connection with his natural self liberates him, and he experiences an intellectual and emotional awakening to his own role in the militant religious and colonialist machine, as well as to his homosexuality. While Lueli is initially described in primitivist terms, these gradually extend to the homoerotic, placing Fortune's position as the white, normative gazer as suspect. Wachman, too, notes that Warner "presents the colonialist discourse of the 'primitive' ironically, introducing and then immediately undercutting stereotypes of class and 'race' upon which imperialist power depends" (92). In this way, Warner carefully satirizes Fortune's self-realization. The author constantly mocks and rewrites binaries of self and other. Indeed Warner's ambiguity about the ethics of her character results in Fortune's troubling unreliability.

Upon first meeting Lueli, Fortune describes him as a typical white European might—in animalistic terms—and intimates his desire to correct and categorize him as some kind of exotic creature:

> He felt as though he were watching some entirely new kind of being, too spontaneous to be human, too artless to be a monkey, too sensitive to be a bird or squirrel or lizard; and he wished that he had been more observant of creation, so that he could find out what it was that Lueli resembled. Only some women, happy in themselves and in their love, will show to a lover or husband this kind of special grace. (21)

Almost immediately, then, Lueli is laid out for Fortune's private, inspecting gaze, even masculinist as he wonders about Lueli's physical charm—and all this while Warner's narrator looks on with some derision at Fortune's own lack of self-scrutiny.[6] Fortune refers to Lueli as "the true Polynesian type, slender-boned and long-limbed" (21) while also noting that "the boy looked very refined for one who had been so recently a heathen" (22). Fortune acts as an anthropologist set out to catalog all the plant and animal species he stumbles upon in the "wild." His voyeuristic investigation of Lueli's "elegance" draws him to the conclusion that "it seemed as though he had been decorated for no better reason than the artist's pleasure" (23). The question is: whose behavior indicates hedonism here? Fortune's romanticizing gaze places him in the position of a repressed, yet overemotional, proto-Romantic artist whose appreciative response to the beauty of the physical world is just waiting to be realized in this intoxicating primitive place. His deep connection with the primitive here comes as a result of Lueli's objectification as a kind of noble savage, an intriguing new racial type awaiting his expert, imperialist classification.

However, Warner's queering of Fortune—and his "housewifely mind" (211)—destabilizes him as a legitimate instrument of a masculinist British Empire and calls into question whether Warner is actually being ironic in her depiction of Fanua as an especially sensual and free locale. Fortune repeatedly denies the possibility of homoerotic desire on his part, in spite of the fact that he was a boy whom, the narrator remembers, read books "secretly and rather bashfully, because [they were] book[s] for girls" (89). He literally flees the presence of the young women of the island, calling them "nymphs" (28) and "young whores" (29), and feels, "he could have endured even twice as many girls as the price of being soothed by one such boy" (30). He primps himself as a supposed measure to garner respect from the natives. Still, he initially refuses to succumb to Lueli's oiling of his body after a bathing because he cannot submit himself to "their way...his views on oiling were inherent and unshakable. They were inherent in the very marrow of his backbone, which was a British one. Oiling, and all that sort of thing, was effeminate, unbecoming, and probably vicious" (93). But for someone who, before he met the fascinating Lueli, "was rather careless about his appearance," his present behavior enacts that of a man more interested in attracting a (male) lover: "he made his toilet with extraordinary circumspection and deliberation" (38).

Fortune soon realizes "a curious sensation...he was [a] man of stone" (38) whose rigid self-definition denotes a great deal of anxiety. He strives to maintain a typically masculine, stone-like exterior self while his true, inner self bursts forth with longing, finally cracking the outer construction in eruptive homosexual panic. An anxious moment occurs just after scolding and threatening Lueli ("For I cannot allow myself to love a boy who flouts me"!) for foiling his attempts to Christianize him (40). It is in the consequent connection with Lueli's body that Fortune begins to realize the truth of Lueli's (and his own) humanity:

> Now he spoke almost pleadingly...for his hand was no longer stone but flesh and blood...suddenly, and completely to his surprise, he found himself convulsed with laughter...so utterly unexpected, so perfectly natural, rapt him into an ecstasy of appreciation...He had never been so real before...he squealed as he fetched his breath. (42-3)

Warner reveals moments of *jouissance* for Fortune, in spite of his rigid religious life, suggesting that he might actually be more like his perception of the natives than he realizes.

Following this almost orgasmic episode, Fortune experiences a moment of repose. He releases himself against a tree to enjoy a moment in which to "look...at his thoughts" (43) and see himself more clearly. This erotically charged instance borders on the post-coital, and represents a particular example of the way in which reconnection with the maternal utopia enacts what feminist critic Gloria Anzaldúa calls "the space in-between from which to think" (172), the moment that arrests time and offers personal (and possibly communal) transformation. In Fortune's realization that, "'I do feel most extraordinarily happy. And as mild as milk—as mothers' milk'" (45). In his newfound sense of happiness, he appears as tranquil as a child at his mother's breast. At length, "he was profoundly satisfied, and rather pleased with himself, with his new self, that is." In this instance of (perhaps) serious alteration, Fortune fuels his contentment with his self-recognition.

At this point in the novel, we are still not sure of the validity of Fortune's self-transformation. He still views Lueli as an object to be analyzed for his own personal benefit. Fortune begins to fear that he has finally lost Lueli's affection to the idol he ordered the boy to destroy: "A frightful imagination took possession of him: that Lueli was become like his idol, a handsome impassive thing of brown wood, that had ears and heard not, that had no life in its heart" (118). His urgency is augmented by the chaotic arrival of an earthquake, which laughably heaves his beloved "harmonium" on top of him (119). Yet even in the midst of the debilitating forces of nature, Fortune can only think regretfully of his relationship with Lueli. He laments, "I know now he never cared for me" just before Lueli becomes his knight in shining armor by rescuing him from the heaving harmonium and the festering fire. And here again, Warner stresses the "horribly comic" (121) situation at hand in narrating Fortune's pathetic self-indulgence and total ineffectuality in the face of disaster, further destabilizing him as a representative of British class and gender normalcy or pre-eminence.[7]

It soon becomes evident that the accoutrements of "civilized" culture no longer have meaning within this primitive space. The order of British Empire is most explicitly undercut in the text once Fortune's watch stops functioning: "It had stopped...his last link with European civilization had been snapped...[which] upset him horribly. He felt frightened, he felt as small and as desperate as a child lost" (142). Significantly, it is at this juncture in the novel that Fortune begins his process of metamorphoses, yet for the moment, he cannot feel comfort in the unfolding chaos. First he must reset his watch, although this gesture ultimately highlights his anxious feeling of failure: "It began to tick, innocently, obediently. It had set out on its fraudulent career" (143).

Warner also reveals, in Fortune's panicked reaction to the earthquake and the ensuing eruption of the island volcano, his fear of a Freudian oceanic, evidencing his dread of female sexuality. In response to the shock of the earthquake, Fortune and Lueli create a haven of protection in one another's presence, a contact zone that wards off the danger of nature unleashed: "Mr. Fortune had forgotten the sea. Now he remembered what he had read in books of adventure as a boy: how after an earthquake comes a tidal wave...[and he and Lueli] sat side by side, holding on to one another" (122). More than the actual ocean, the volcanic vigor beneath the sea comes to represent Fortune's terror in the prospect of a kind of traditionally feminine power—"the foundations of the great deep, into an unimaginable hell of energy and black burning" (126)—that ironically parallels the release of his own truer self. The gaping mouth of the volcano is analogous to the fearful orifices of womanhood Fortune would surely flee, much like the "nymphs" and "whores" who live on the island.[8]

A case in point occurs later, when Fortune inspects the crater while "grasping for breath and cowed by the frantic beating of his heart, which did not seem to belong to him, behaving like some wild animal" (213). He remembers the story of "the woman Kapiolani, the Christian convert of Hawaii" (214) whose faith was stronger than his own. He also evokes the story the Fire-goddess Pele, whose dangerous female sexuality causes him anxiety: "Pele fell asleep...to dream;

snarling to herself, and hotly, voluptuously, obscurely triumphing in a dream what her next awakening would be" (215). As he looks down at the crater, he notes that "by night the spectacle might have had a sort of Medusa's head beauty, for ever wakeful...and dangerous" (218). Fortune seems to equate female sexual energy with the impending re-convergence with the maternal body that he cannot escape: "Everywhere in the woods was the odour of mortality; it was sweet to him, like a *home-coming*" (219; my emphasis).

Fortune simultaneously dreads and welcomes this homecoming. While he fears the inevitability of the fire, he is also drawn to this power; he experiences conflicting urges to both reintegrate with the maternal body and abandon or abject that body: "Though the next moment might engulf him he was going to make the most of this...he sat down again and relinquished himself to an entire and passive contemplation, almost lulled by the inexhaustible procession of fire and smoke, warming his mind at the lonely terrific beauty of a mountain burning by night amid an ocean" (126-7). His encounter with this wholly primal power further renders him a changed man: "It was as though the earthquake had literally shaken his wits. All his recollections were dislodged and tumbled together" (135). Bruce Knoll remarks that Warner "sets up nature as a female ethic completely outside the patriarchy" (355). At this moment in *Mr. Fortune's Maggot,* Warner uses the chaotic power of Nature as the driving force of Fortune's transformation through a maternally-connected experience of wholeness. Nature's call "implies a relationship of reciprocity" (357) that enacts interplay between and among inner and outer self, self and other, and ultimately, self and community.[9]

Throughout the novel then, Fortune intermittently embraces the utopian moment of interconnectivity. At a party to celebrate the natives' safety after the volcanic eruption, he begins to relax: "Mr. Fortune was much happier than he expected to be. He was now engaged in growing a beard, and freed from any obligation to convert his housemates...he found their society very agreeable" (151). He buries the "bones" of his harmonium, lamp, sewing-machine, all signs of his former middle-class domesticity and civilized life. He wears a floral crown as he asks Lueli to remember him, and this seems to be his moment of supreme happiness: "Fortune walked home with Lueli by moonlight...A night bird was calling among the trees—a soft breathy note like an also flute—and the roof of the hut shone in the moonlight" (244). The imagery of domesticity is not entirely expunged from Fortune's association with the idyllic primitive space, but it is transformed, for here Fortune experiences the rapture of a romantic moment with his newfound love, and both natural and domestic worlds reflect the light of his joy.

Warner's depiction of a kind of Edenic primitivism, a common blunder for modernist writers, cannot entirely escape Gay Wachman's disapproval, even in its clever response to Robert Louis Stevenson's life and writings.[10] Warner's intersubjective moment is always in collusion with the primitive present. As early as the opening passages of the novel, Fortune remembers his English past and thinks, "And now he scarcely knew himself for happiness. The former things were passed away...the bank...There had passed the worst days of his life...And now he was at Fanua, and at his side squatted Lueli" (54). Very soon after he settles on Fanua, he contemplates the joyful power of the present moment in nature: "he went for a long rejoicing walk, a walk full of the most complicated animal ecstasy" and "he felt a violent sympathy with all the greenery that seemed to be wearing the deepened colour of intense gratification" (51). At this point he recognizes his liberated, "authentic" self, or "a secret core of delight, a sense of truancy, of freedom" (52). Once he begins to enjoy oiling with Lueli, he sees that, "It did him a great deal of good, and it improved his appearance ten-fold...he discovered that somehow his expression has changed" (95). This newfound bliss is a result of Fortune's successful convergence with that primitive locale and all the openness it embodies for this formerly stilted English banker.

However, Warner examines how this British character responds to his own complicity in imperialism by narrating that encounter almost chiefly from that British subject's perspective. And, her narrator presents Fortune ambiguously and ironically. Indeed, Fortune cannot always seem to reconcile his own imperialist Englishness with the emerging sense of wholeness in his desire for primitive beauty and integrity. At the moment of staring into the crater of the volcano, Fortune reveals his fear of the connection between the primitive and the depraved in his realization that, "He had no thoughts, no feelings. What he had seen was something older than the earth; but vestigial, and to the horror of the sun what the lizard is to the dragon: degenerate" (218). Rigby notes, "It is also a product of Warner's modernism which presents Fanua as a primitive and natural alternative to a rigid and all-consuming Western culture, and it can certainly be argued that the integrity of the island suffers from her conscious artistic decision not to explore the island society in any depth" (243). It is true that at no point in the novel do we receive the benefit of narration from an islander's consciousness.

However, Fortune is consistently incapable of asserting the supposed superiority of his own culture over the more "primitive." Warner's own critique, through her narrator's presentation of colonialism's primitivizing gaze, denotes Fortune's "increasing critical consciousness of the meanings of militant Christianity and imperialism" (Wachman 84). For example, Lueli's music, despite Fortune's "musical accomplishments, his cultivated taste, and enough grasp of musical theory to be able to transpose any hymn into its nearly related keys, was not so truly musical as Lueli" (69). Most importantly, Fortune finds that he respects the natives (although almost begrudgingly) too much to continue in his quest to "civilize" them with religious doctrine: "Not that he loved his flock less. Rather he loved them more, and to his love was added (and here was the rub) a considerable amount of esteem" (99).

Finally, Fortune realizes, as a result of his further emotional development through his reconnection with his preoriginary self in the primitive space, that imperialism underlies his religion, which "is torments, wounds, mutilation, and death…It is strife—and endless strife—it is bewilderment and fear and trembling. It is despair" (112). The complete reevaluation of Fortune's surroundings and his identity results in his loss of faith in an imperialist god. Just as he is about to disparage Lueli's beloved idol, he recognizes the emptiness of that scolding, and narrates a deep criticism of empire itself: "He felt a deep reluctance in saying it. It seemed ungentlemanly to have such a superior invulnerable God, part of that European conspiracy which opposes gunboats to canoes and rifles to bows and arrows, which showers death from the mountains upon Indian villages, which rounds up the negro into an empire and tricks them of his patrimony" (140). Moreover, "the God who had walked with him upon the island was gone...Mr. Fortune no longer believed in a God" (147). He rejects that oppressive dogma and finds legitimacy in Lueli's faith in his idol, conceding that "Lueli had lost something real" (148). Then Fortune compassionately carves Lueli a new idol. In Rigby's words, "Timothy finally understands that not only does European colonisation succeed through the destruction of colonial difference, but that Europe is also destroying itself through its intolerance" (230). I add that it is Fortune's recognition of his own, more whole self, accomplished largely through this measure of commiseration with "native" experience, that results in his amelioration.

Through his primitive connection to his own "authentic" state of consciousness, similar to Anzaldúa's notion of "*mestiza* consciousness, *una concienciade mujer*...of the Borderlands" (77), Warner opens up the possibility of Fortune's truly loving another—and a young man at that. Fortune abandons his possessive passion for Lueli and replaces it with the open acceptance that Lueli had always shown him "because [Lueli] was incapable of feeling that sad, civilized and proprietary love which is anxious and predatory and spoil-sport" (237). Again, it is this newfound sense of sympathy that allows Fortune to imagine an anti-imperial future with Lueli. And it is the third person narration which allows us to see Fortune's recognition more deeply.

Although Warner participates in the ideology of primitivist romance, she also complicates it through the novel's elegiac, political end. Nigel Rigby notes, "empire was simply a part of life in in-between-the-wars Britain, whatever one's social class, and that all writers were inevitably exposed to the wide range of imperial narrative at the time" (225). The same holds true for Warner. Gay Wachman writes, "Mr. Fortune's desolation represents mourning and loss as well as nostalgia for a prewar paradise on a tropical island" (97). The most compelling interruption of Fortune's Edenic state is the impending war. Although the earthquake and volcano could also be read as signals of the cataclysm of war far away from the shores of Fanua, Warner's novel incorporates more pointed references to empire. When Fortune contemplates his legacy on the island, he regrets that "there would soon be plenty of white men to frighten the children of Fanua, to bring them galvanized iron and law-courts and commerce and industry and bicycles and patent medicines and American alarm clocks, besides the blessing of religion" (233). The imperialist regime will continue to invade this paradise, but it seems that Fortune will have no part in that process. Once he has boarded the launch out of Fanua, the secretary on board "immediately began to tell [him] about the Great War," to which Fortune admits, "'Of course I have heard nothing of all this'" and even that he "could not yet gather who was fighting who, still less what they were fighting about" (247-8). The novel concludes with an image of the fading dream of the primitive utopian state: "Meanwhile the island of Fanua was sinking deeper into the Pacific Ocean...Everything that was real, everything that was significant, had gone down with the island of Fanua and was lost for ever" (249).

Fortune must become separated from that space by the end of the novel, so his restorative reconnection is short-lived, however his conversion is life-affirming and possibly transcendent. Soon after Fortune writes his resignation letter with a "reed pen," the narrator surveys Lueli's appearance through Fortune's perspective: "Never before had he been so beautiful, nor moved so lithely, nor sprawled so luxuriously on the warm grass. Sleek, languid and glittering, he was like a snake that had achieved its new skin" (203). The primitive environs of the island of Fanua afford this image of rebirth, which extends to Fortune's future. Fortune can recall his experience, as if the profound reciprocal murmur between mother and child, as he lies "in a timeless world, listening. Then, at last, he heard and was released—for what he heard, a murmur, a wandering wreath of sound, was Lueli talking softly to his god" (229). The aural quality of the murmur occurs at the instance of Fortune's initial assimilation with the utopian moment in the natural splendor of the island:

"Though [the clouds] were silent he imagined then a voice, an enormous soft murmur, sinking and swelling as they tumbled and evolved and amassed" (51). This sensual interplay between present self and child self recreates fleeting moments of wholeness, choran moments, that may be brought into the future.

Warner's evocation of Fanua as a place of restoration allows it to become a catalyst for both personal and universal renewal (or a kind of spiritual, communal "fortune") rather than exploitation.[11] Warner's depiction perpetuates the primitivist stereotype of what Anne McClintock describes as "anachronistic space,"[12] yet Fortune's experience of these environs creates the possibility that he will continue this new mode of being in his future life back on the island of Great Britain, as evidenced by his decision to leave his missionary post. Knoll's commentary applies to the modernist choran moment and its aesthetic of interconnectivity represented in *Mr. Fortune's Maggot*:

> Although Townsend Warner's answer may not be the final one, she shows up a way to approach life, which lies not in attempting to control our environment, on in passively accepting it, but rather in understanding its terms, and allowing ourselves to be transformed. (362)

Warner also presents Fortune as one who allows himself to become transformed by a new understanding of his interrelationship with a greater community. Although Warner hints that the process of building a bridge from self to other to community may be complicated by war, nonetheless the (re)production of Mr. Timothy Fortune's genuine self has transpired, and he will never be the same.

Despite the eloquent and groundbreaking work of literary scholars and writers like Toni Morrison,[13] a profound difficulty remains in transcending modernism's protracted views of primitivism. I don't want to claim here that Warner was particularly conscious of or even completely untainted in her portrayal of the choran moment. Rather my point is that as readers in the present day, we may, without claiming an author is entirely innocent, victimized, masterful or pandering, recognize the possibility of a counternarrative enacted in her novel. What, then, are we to do with a novel that offers up the possibility of connection between self and other, but uses primitivism to realize that vision?

Indeed the development of modernism itself depended upon white culture's appropriation of primitivist stereotypes. AnaLouise Keating suggests another possibility: "[T]o transform walls into bridges, into spiraling paths from self to other, from other to self" (11). In the practice of building bridges, we can recognize that "spiritual activism begins with the personal yet moves outward, acknowledging our radical interconnectedness" (18). Timothy Fortune begins the process by which we might, as readers,[14] turn from patriarchal and racist ideological assumptions to "experience the world as unknown and unexpected and to create out of that opening-up-to the presence of another" (Shloss 15). In the work of Sylvia Townsend Warner, a white, lesbian, British Communist woman writer whose subject positions have also (in part) traditionally been othered, readers of the present and future can catch a glimpse at the possibly redemptive choran moment[15] and thereby begin building bridges to interconnective community.

Works Cited

Anzaldúa, Gloria. *Borderlands/La Frontera: The New Mestiza*. San Francisco: Aunt Lute Books, 1987.

Baker, Jr., Houston A. *Modernism and the Harlem Renaissance*. Chicago: U of Chicago Press, 1987.

Barkan, Elazar and Ronald Bush, eds. *Prehistories of the Future: The Primitivist Project and the Culture of Modernism,* Stanford: Stanford UP, 1995.

Bhabha, Homi K. "The Commitment to Theory." *Nation and Narration*. London and New York: Routledge, 1990: 18-28.

Derrida, Jacques. *On the Name*. ed. Thomas Dutoit, trans. David Wood, John P. Leavy, Jr., and Ian McLeod. Stanford, CA: Stanford University Press, 1993.

Hackett, Robin. *Sapphic Primitivism: Productions of Race, Class, and Sexuality in Key Works of Modern Fiction*. New Brunswick: Rutgers UP, 2004.

Harman, Claire. *Sylvia Townsend Warner: A Biography*. London: Chatto and Windus, Ltd., 1989.

Huggins, Nathan Irvin. *Harlem Renaissance*. New York: Oxford UP, 1971.

Kaplan, E. Ann. *Looking for the Other: Feminism, Film, and the Imperial Gaze*. New York: Routledge, 1997.

Knoll, Bruce. ""An Existence Doled Out': Passive resistance as a dead end in Sylvia Townsend Warner's *Lolly Willowes*." *Twentieth Century Literature* 39.3 (Fall 1993): 344-63.

Keating, AnaLouise. "Charting Pathways, Marking Thresholds…A Warning, An Introduction." *This Bridge We Call Home: Radical Visions for Transformation*. Ed. Gloria E. Anzaldúa and AnaLouise Keating. New York and London: Routledge, 2002: 6-20.

Kristeva, Julia. *A Question of Subjectivity: An Interview*. rpt. *Modern Literary Theory: A Reader*. ed. Phillip Rice and Patricia Waugh. New York: Arnold, 1996.

Lacan, Jacques. "The Mirror Stage as Formative of the Function of the I as revealed in Psychoanalytic Experience" Alan Sheridan, Trans., *Ecrits, A Selection* (1949): 1-7.

Lemke, Sieglinde. *Primitivist Modernism: Black Culture and the Origins of Transatlantic Modernism*. Oxford and New York: Oxford UP, 1998.

Maxwell, William. *Letters: Sylvia Townsend Warner*. New York: Viking Press, 1983.

Mehew, Ernest, Ed. *Selected Letters of Robert Louis Stevenson*. New Haven and London: Yale UP, 1997.

McClintock, Anne. *Imperial Leather: Race, Gender and Sexuality in the Colonial Contest*. New York: Routledge, 1995.

Morrison, Toni. *Playing in the Dark: Whiteness and the Literary Imagination.* Cambridge: Harvard UP, 1992.

Oliver, Kelly, Ed. *The Portable Kristeva.* New York: Routledge, 1996.

Pratt, Mary Louise. *Imperial Eyes: Travel Writing and Transculturation.* London and New York: Routledge, 1992.

Rigby, Nigel. "'Not a Good Place for Deacons': The South Seas, Sexuality and Modernism in Sylvia Townsend Warner's *Mr. Fortune's Maggot.*" *Modernism and Empire,* Ed. and Intro., Howard J. Booth and Nigel Rigby. Manchester: Manchester UP, 2000: 224-78.

Shloss, Carol. *In Visible Light: Photography and the American Writer, 1840-1940.* New York: Oxford UP, 1987.

Showalter, Elaine. *Sexual Anarchy; Gender and Culture at the Fin de Siècle.* New York: Penguin Books, 1991.

Wachman, Gay. *Lesbian Empire: Radical Crosswriting in the Twenties.* New Brunswick, NJ: Rutgers UP, 2001.

Warner, Sylvia Townsend. *Mr. Fortune's Maggot.* [1927] London: Virago Limited, 1978.

University of New Hampshire

Notes

[1] See Nathan Irvin Huggins, Houston A. Baker, Jr, Ann E. Kaplan, and Sieglinde Lemke, for examples.

[2] The quote marks in my title recognize "primitivism" as a historically racist notion deeply implicated with imperialism. Primarily beginning in the mid-nineteenth century, cultural ideologists polarized categories of "primitive" and "civilized" in order to justify an often brutal imperialism: the assumption that "savages" needed to be civilized contributed to notions of the "white man's burden." For more, see Elazar Barkan and Ronald Bush (2). In my work, I consider primitivism through the lens of Homi Bhabha's idea of the third space afforded by the hybridity of binaries like black and white. My larger work examines this third space's "open endedness" (Lemke 150) or "contact zone" (Pratt, *Imperial Eyes* 4) in representative visual and written modernist texts.

[3] Julia Kristeva subversively transformed Lacanian philosophy into feminist theory. Kristeva reinvents the imaginary realm of Lacan's mirror stage as the "chora," in which the infant's babblings to her mother and herself (which the child cannot yet distinguish between) are

understood as a connection or return to the semiotic, prelanguage, pregendered and maternally bonded state of existence.

[4] He strives to keep all under control upon his arrival, yet his sexuality is unstable from the beginning.

[5] Similarly, McClintock examines the crossroads of class, gender and race in imperialism and designates the gendering of unknown lands as a "porno-tropics" (*Imperial Leather* 21-4) as the imperialist males' fearful gesture of dominance in the face of the unknown maternal figure.

[6] As Rigby states, "her narrative voices eschew the possession of the islanders' thoughts which is typical of imperialist writing" (228).

[7] Warner critiques the supposed legitimacy of the marriage institution as well, not only through Fortune's homosexuality and implicit rejection of hetero-normativity, but also in her own life. See Claire Harman's biography.

[8] As Elaine Showalter relevantly states, "If the rebellious New Woman—the 'shrieking sister'—or the prostitute could be turned into a silent body to be observed, measured, and studied, her resistance to convention could be treated as a scientific anomaly or a problem to be solved by medicine" (*Sexual Anarchy* 127-8). French doctor Récamier invented the speculum in 1845, while the American gynecologist Marion Sims "experienced himself as a 'colonizing and conquering hero" [when using the speculum for the first time, rejoicing,] "I saw everything as no man had ever seen before'" (129). Timothy Fortune seems to exhibit the residual values of Victorian sexuality.

[9] Knoll is referring to Warner's first novel, *Lolly Willowes*, but his claim is equally true for this.

[10] Aside from Warner's more obvious references to Robert Louis Stevenson's adventure stories (ie. *Treasure Island*) and his own retirement on the island of Samoa, I perceive a connection between the novel's title and a comment RLS made in a letter to Henry James. Ernest Mehew notes that for the duration of his stay in Bournemouth from July 1884 to August 1887, RLS "lived the life of a chronic invalid, spending much of his time in bed plagued by colds and hemorrhages: a life that he was later to sum up in a famous phrase as that of 'a pallid brute that lived in Skerryvore like a weevil in a biscuit'" (267). If Timothy Fortune is supposed to represent Stevenson in any way, then it seems that this more well-known definition of "maggot" could be another subtle clue to that connection.

[11] Wachman provides a favorable final assessment of *Mr. Fortune's Maggot*: the novel "succeeds in holding politics and perverse desire, primitivism and satire, material specificity, fantasy, and elegy in a fragile, fleeting equilibrium that [allows] its representation of innocent pederasty [to] continue to delight" (71).

[12] McClintock discusses the central feature of nineteenth century industrial capitalism as the assumption that images of "non-European time...were systematically evoked to identify what was historically new about industrial modernity" (40). The island of Fanua, as Robin Hackett argues, embodies such a place: "[It is] marked as a primitive place by the fact that Mr. Fortune's watch...stops running shortly after his arrival" (93).

[13] Morrison writes about this phenomenon without ever using the word "primitivism": The principle reason these matters loom large for me is that I do not have quite the same access to these traditionally useful constructs of blackness. Neither blackness nor "people of color" stimulates in me notions of excessive, limitless love, anarchy, or routine dread. I cannot rely on these

metaphorical shortcuts because I am a black writer struggling with and through language that can powerfully evoke and enforce hidden signs of racial superiority, cultural hegemony, and dismissive "othering" of people and language which are by no means marginal or already and completely known and knowable in my work...The kind of work I have always wanted to do requires me to learn how to maneuver ways to free up that language from its sometimes sinister, frequently lazy, almost always predictable employment of racially informed and determined chains. (*Playing in the Dark* x-xi)

[14] The implications of ethical literary analysis, involving recognition and acceptance of interconnection among humanity as well as the empathetic practice emerging from this understanding, rest upon those scholars who read, examine, and teach literature. By embracing the otherness within, recognizing and accepting one another (without criticism) as selves in process, Warner began the project of a just transcendence of ideological and historical brutalities. As recipients of this literary tradition, we might continue this project in our readings of modernism today.

[15] Kristeva uses the idea of the chora as a space to open possibility, both political and cultural. See note 3 above.

CHAPTER 6

"This was a Lesson in History": Sylvia Townsend Warner, George Townsend Warner and the Matter of History

Rosemary Sykes

"If story-telling had not appealed to her more," suggests William Maxwell, "Sylvia Townsend Warner might have been a formidable historian." Indeed, to the privileged children of Britain's preparatory schools the name Townsend Warner *is* associated first and foremost with history. For even today, nearly 90 years after the death of George Townsend Warner pupils still compete in the annual Townsend Warner History Competition[1]. George Townsend Warner—son of an Anglican clergyman; sometime fellow of Jesus College, Cambridge; master of the modern side at Harrow School (a school for the brightest sons of the wealthiest families, rivalled only by Eton College)—was also a writer, particularly of history textbooks for use in schools. In his time his teaching was considered outstanding. Apparently, "his advice [was] sought and opinions accepted without discussion" by dons at both Oxford and Cambridge[2]. His daughter, however, was educated at home. As well as being taught by governesses, she claimed to have read everything in the house[3] and often benefited from her father's undivided attention[4]. But Sylvia felt that her *real* education in history came when she was doing background research for *Summer Will Show*. Delving into histories and memoirs written soon after the 1848 Paris Revolt, she found inconsistent dates and incompatible accounts. "This was a lesson in history", she was later to recall, remarking also: "but their prejudices made them what I needed."[5] For one of the ironies when considering the works of both father and daughter is that it was Sylvia (musicologist, creative writer) who handled original manuscripts as she carried out research for the Tudor Church Music Project, and near-contemporary accounts as she researched her novels, whilst her father (historian, purveyor of fact) admits that his skill lay in composition. In *Landmarks of Industrial History* (1899) he asserted that "the novelty of my book lies merely in selection and arrangement"[6]; and the stated aim of *The Groundwork of British History* (1912) (which he co-authored with C.H.K. Marten) was "to trace out the main threads of British history, omitting small and unfruitful details."[7]

The historian Herbert Butterfield writes in the 1920s: "the history of textbooks is really little more than a chart of the past." If Sylvia was used to history of this sort, it is scarcely surprising that her discovery of incompatibilities and prejudices took her aback. One of the books she used was a collection of documents: R.W. Postgate's *Revolutions from 1789 to 1906: Documents*. "Valentine was sure I had a cold coming", Warner wrote in her diary on 16 March 1935, "so I spent the day in bed with Postgate's Revolutionary documents of the 19th Century and my patchwork."[8] Postgate's book is itself a patchwork of sorts, but his preface makes it plain that, though his excerpts are of many types, he has a clear design in mind:

> [This is] not an attempt to depict the course of various arbitrarily selected revolutions in the words of the revolutionaries themselves...The aim of the Editor has been rather to select speeches, posters and articles which show what the revolution "was all about": what ere the principles, the thoughts in their minds, and the phrases they used: and particularly which of their acts became the seeds of future revolution.[9]

Whilst Sylvia, too, recommended an emphasis on principles and thoughts, she was addressing novelists, rather than historians, when she delivered her lecture "The Historical Novel" at the Third Congress of the League of American Writers in New York in 1939.

> The historical novelist cannot dodge the obligation, so it seems to me, of knowing pretty accurately how people clothed their minds. Human nature does not change etc., but human thinking alters a great deal, it is conditioned by what it has been taught, what it believes or disbelieves; what it admires in art or nature; at what age it marries, to what extent it has outwitted the weather...what careers are open to it.[10]

One wonders how much of this her father might have considered as an emphasis on those "small and unfruitful details" he was so anxious to excise, but what Sylvia is actually describing is the uncovering of what we might call a metanarrative, a guiding system of beliefs, a narrative of history as progress. Postgate's collection of documents—primary sources presented as if neutrally—is actually history as a template for "the seeds of future revolution", and the template used is the Communist Manifesto, which he works neatly into his design on page 139: "not only did it turn Socialism forever from the paths of secret conspiracy into those of open propaganda; it gave to it its place in history." Sylvia, therefore, might be seen (in *Summer Will Show*) as giving the manifesto its place in art[11]. But note here how Postgate's editing favours the rhetoric of public record, not private reflection. Even in the presentation of primary sources the historian's aim is a cohesive narrative, not the inconsistencies that gave Sylvia her "lesson in history". George Townsend Warner's aim was not just a cohesive narrative but also to "add value", as it were, to history:

> The value of history as an educational subject, even to the young, cannot, I think, be fully realized, unless some stress is placed upon the sequence of cause and effect, so as to exercise not merely the memory but the reason[12].

Even as he stresses history's "value as an educational subject", Warner seems not to recognise how strongly his own values come through. For the story he narrates, what he describes as "the broadening stream of our national history" (and we shall see shortly the fun his daughter had with streams and history,) is actually empiricist and imperialist: it is the story of Empire. In discussing, for instance, the wars Britain took part in during the mid-eighteenth century, he observes that "this variety of enemies seems to point to Britain's being universally quarrelsome;" nevertheless, "Britain was really only carrying on the struggle with the French which had begun with William III, the object was colonial." Perhaps her father's prose and methods provide the inspiration for Mr Tizard—a character in her story "A Love Match"—who, though "he had every intention of preserving a historian's impartiality" was, nevertheless "infected by the current mood of disliking the French."[13]

I have considered, so far, the teaching of history in the very late-19th and early-20th centuries. Before switching my focus to Sylvia Townsend Warner's thoughts about history and historical novels in the late 1930s and early 1940s, however, I want to make a few observations about the status of historical novels, and Sylvia's use of history in her novels, during the 1920s and 1930s. It is curious, but neither the Oxford nor the Cambridge Companions to English Literature makes any mention of the novels Sylvia wrote after the 1920s. I suspect that this is because they are dismissed as being that dreaded thing "genre fiction" or, more precisely, historical. As Janet Montefiore has put it, "historical novels...are a fairly specialized and obscure variety of fiction." Now whilst this observation may be correct from the perspective of recent literary criticism, this was not the case for those who were reading such novels during the 1920s and 1930s. Academic historians like Herbert Butterfield were stressing the value of historical novels in helping students to develop their "historical imagination"[14]. Or, as GM Trevelyan observed in 1927, "the appeal of History to us all is in the last analysis poetic"[15]. He felt that the history taught for examinations was necessary but that it "tended to diminish the unplumbed and uncharted wastes of history."[16] The pedagogical value of historical novels is apparent from the leaflets published by the Historical Association during the 1920s[17] and from Jonathan Nield's *Guide to the Best Historical Novels and Tales*. Nield states that his work was compiled "partly as an aid to teachers" and that his new, (1929), edition was prompted "by an almost alarming influx in this department of fiction" in "the last year or two". This suggests an upsurge in the writing of historical novels even before the left-wing novelists of the 1930s moved towards portraying current events in—as Montefiore and others have suggested— Aesopian language. The two novels Sylvia wrote during the 1930s (*Summer Will Show, After the Death of Don Juan*) are often read (accurately, interestingly) as a coded commentary on contemporary events. But is that to say that Sylvia used history solely to critique the present? At least two things would suggest not. Firstly—and this is something which frequently goes unremarked—history was deployed to great effect in her early novels, too. In *Lolly Willowes* there is a cunningly constructed family history[18]. And *Mr Fortune's Maggot*, dismissed by C.H. Rickword in the *Calendar of Modern Letters* as being set in the "never never Islands", is actually set in a never-again land. As the missionary Timothy Fortune leaves the Pacific Island of Fanua, he is immediately told that in the Great War "the Germans crucified Belgian children". Not only is Mr Fortune exiled from "everything that was real, everything that was significant, gone down with the island...and lost forever." His presence has also changed the island irrevocably, leaving pencil sharpeners, measuring tapes and other such (symbolic) trappings of modernity. Note here how Sylvia has used details that her father might have considered "small and unfruitful" to pointed effect. And this is also a devastating critique of her father's preferred metanarrative of Empire.

Yet although Sylvia does seem to use her novels as a critique of recent events, she was quite scathing about many of the historical novels of the 1930s. In the lecture she gave in New York she observes that whilst in "traditional historical novels" there had been a class distinction—"the upper class characters were fully period" but "servants and peasants...had scarcely a period rag to cover them"—there had been a recent "Revolt against this":

> *All* the characters in historical novels are of the present day, contemporary in speech, in behaviour, in motive, in psychology. But the talisman is not infallible, and these characters straight out of modern life may make up a perfectly lifeless book. There must, it seems, be some recognition of history in the historical novel[19].

And so, having suggested that to historians (if not to literary critics) the historical novel was seen as an important pedagogical tool, I want to conclude by considering Sylvia's recognition of history, and her barbed parody of historiography, in *The Corner That Held Them*, the work that she wrote whilst England was (again) at War.

The "small and unfruitful details" that George Townsend Warner omitted became, as we have seen, the stock-in-trade of his daughter. In her earlier novels playfully miscegenetic lists litter her works, laced with malice aforethought. As well as the gifts left on Fanua, we have lists such as this one from *Lolly Willowes*, a list of institutions the heroine feels she must "needs forgive" before she can forgive her family:

> Society, the Law, the Church, the History of Europe, the Old Testament, great-great-aunt Salome and her prayerbook, the Bank of England, Prostitution…and half a dozen other useful props of civilisation[20].

In *The Corner That Held Them*, it is Sylvia's mock-inventorial style (deliberately conflating unlikely bedfellows) that becomes her novel's structure. She wrote (delightedly) to friends that "my new novel has no plot", and indeed it is episodic in structure. It clearly confused her British publisher, who requested cuts, particularly of all the politicking that her nuns got up to. In the novel it is Oby, the nunnery, that is both locus and focus of the book. The nuns come and go, but Oby remains. And it is this emphasis on the many small happenings over at least 30 years within one place that makes me think that Sylvia had anticipated the coming of the soap opera to Britain, where our native soaps have such titles as *Coronation Street*; *Emmerdale Farm*; and *Brookside*. Place and geography are closely bound up with time and people. So let us return to George Townsend Warner's geographical trope of "the broadening stream of our British history" and also to Sylvia's first impressions of historical novels:

had usually long and frequent descriptions of scenery—I supposed in order that the author might have a spell of taking it easy. Oaks and brooks get along through the centuries without much fuss about being "period"[21].

In *The Corner That Held Them* Sylvia writes about a brook—the Waxle Stream—that is in a constant state of flux. But with the Waxle Stream Sylvia was not lazily adding local colour without the need for adding period detail. This stream becomes a metaphor for both flux and the passage of time. In this it is like the Hog Trail, the causeway that rises above the periodic floods caused by the Waxle Stream. The Hog Trail is not merely the Isle of Oby's connexion to the wider world, it is evidence of "man's will to thwart nature" and, through folk memory, it is a metaphor for the presence of the past in the present. It is associated with invasion and conquest. When first mentioned—as Sylvia is narrating events in the twelfth century—it is a link with the time before the Norman Conquest: it was "made long before the first de Bazingham came into England." As the narrative moves to the fourteenth century, however, the Hog Trail's time line stretches still further back, to the Viking invasions of the east coast. With this dual movement in time, with the Hog Trail's stretching further back as the narrative moves forward in time, it becomes the symbol of the time, and indeed the place, in which Sylvia wrote. Europe was at war and Sylvia, living on the South coast of England, wrote beneath skies "very noisy with bombers"[22]. Flying through the air with weapons, "man's will to thwart nature" had taken a cruel new turn, yet the natural cycle continued; two days before she started writing "a story about a medieval nunnery to be entirely taken up with their monetary difficulties", she noted in her diary that "the wind is pure east, the moon is in her first quarter, we are at war." The moon waxed, even as Britain's fortunes waned. It is, then, perhaps unsurprising that the stream Sylvia described, and which inspired many of the projected titles for the novel[23]—Shadows on a River; A Slow Stream; A Winter Island; The Winter's Island; Time Like a River; Above Flood Level—is a small yet unpredictable one. It forms a stark contrast to "the broadening stream of our national history." Was it, perhaps, also a deliberate riposte to her father?

When she writes about the effects of the Black Death—"in one house, every monk had died. In another every monk but one"—she is actually quoting from one of her father's books, although she has removed the place names he gave[24]. Perhaps such "small and unfruitful details" have no place in a novel about the past? It is a provocative thought, and one that I wish to leave unresolved. Nevertheless, this novel is far more than wartime England projected back onto medieval England. The novel that she described as "A purely Marxian account of nuns" and "not in any way a historical novel, it has no plot, no thesis[25]" (observe the contradiction of describing it to one person as being "Marxian" whilst insisting to another that "it has no thesis") is also about the matter of, the instability of, history itself. In it Sylvia displays a sophisticated grasp of historiography, of writing, and thinking about, how history is written, what it is based on.

The novel begins in high genre-fiction mode, as Alianor de Retteville lies in bed with her lover:

> She did not speak. She had nothing to say. He did not speak either. They were not alone, for in a corner of the room an old woman sat spinning, but she was no more than the bump and purr of her wheel (1[26]).

What a curious place for a Marxian account of nuns' financial difficulties to begin! And what a vivid picture, implying that the lovers had no need for speech because they too, like the spinning wheel, communicated in the language of "bump and purr". The erotic languor is rudely shattered by murder, as Alianor's husband and cousins sweep in to remove this stain upon the family name. But it is not just Giles, the lover, who must be killed. The old woman, the spinster, must be silenced and, with a "so much for you Dame Bawd!" the possible source of gossip is thrown down the stairs to her death.

Brian de Retteville later repents these deeds and founds the nunnery by way of atonement (how ironic that a nunnery should be conceived by an act of carnality). But it is Dame Bawd who intrigues. Personified thus, she is far more than an anonymous woman; she becomes the figure of domestic tales, of the mother tongue, of the oral tradition, of the material that eludes the "official" documentary record on which history is based. Later in the novel Sylvia will give us accounts of nuns frustrated by their inability to speak Latin and of a poet mocked for writing in his mother tongue. Sylvia has much to say about literary history as well as (for want of a better term) history history.

History history swiftly comes to the fore, as Sylvia fills in the years between the nunnery's creation in the twelfth century and the fourteenth century. Observing—tongue firmly in cheek—that "A good convent should have no history. Its life is hid with Christ above." (7)Sylvia proceeds to write the convent's history, condensing the passing of more than a century as she parodies the annals (lists of dates with an occasional important, usually awful, event written beside them) and chronicles (which introduce a certain element of narrative, as if to tell a story, but still break off *in medias res*) which she doubtless encountered amongst the musical manuscripts she worked on in cathedral archives. And thus:

> In 1297 the bailiff was taken in an act of carnality with a cow. Both he and the cow were duly executed for the crime, but this was not enough to avert the wrath of heaven. That autumn and for three autumns following there was a murrain among the cattle. (11)

A note here on cause and effect: that which, in George Townsend Warner's view, added value to history. Sylvia is at play here, knowing that, in thirteenth-century England, God was (ultimately) both cause of, and authority for, all action. And the Devil was his necessary counterpart in this. In this premodern frame of reference the act of carnality (with the cow) is seen as an act of the Devil (who is the ultimate cause of all such wrongdoings). This misdemeanour requires a retributive act of divine wrath, ergo the cattle plague (the final effect). But consider it also, as Sylvia would have done, from a twentieth-century perspective. The Devil and God are eliminated from the equation, leaving us with, implicitly, act of carnality (cause), cattle plague (effect), suggesting the possibility of sexually transmitted diseases. It is a small and wicked point, swiftly made, swiftly passed over, for soon it is "1345, when Prioress Isabella choked on a plum-stone" whence follow "four ambling years of having no history, save for a plague of caterpillars." Caterpillars apart, those "four ambling years of having no history" suggest, simultaneously, both that the nunnery was being very good (how dull!), its history safely "hid with Christ above", and also that bizarre feature of the annals: the dates that have no events written beside them (signifiers without signifieds, as Hayden White puts it).

Echoes of this bravura pastiche of historiography are found throughout the remainder of the novel. There is much about the nun's monetary troubles, but whilst Sylvia might have seen this as part of a "Marxian" approach, it is also an accurate reflection of the documentation available for this period. We know little of the lives of individuals in religious orders, but their account books remain. And we are shown just how inaccurate written records may be, how they are not always the unproblematical resources that some historians might take them to be.

In the episode entitled "Chapter IX, The Fish Pond (July 1374-September 1374)" (the chapter headings are textbook-like) we see an episode in history—a murder—which, though anything but good, remains hidden "with Christ above" and also from the Bishop. As Bishop Walter records his views on the nuns and their finances, he views Dame Alice (murderess) as "a plain honest good woman" and "he noted and underlined her desire to leave Oby for some simple, God-fearing nunnery where she could live as inconspicuously as possible."(181) And as we consider that it is records such as this that become the basis of history, let us also note a point to be borne in mind by palaeographers: "his handwriting grew neater as his mistrust and indignation grew." (180)

To return to the words of William Maxwell: "if story-telling had not appealed to her more, Sylvia Townsend Warner might have been a formidable historian". I suggest that she *was* a formidable historian, one whose understanding and use of storytelling reveals the fictiveness of any single, historical "real". In Sylvia's fiction we are shown, playfully, with Sylvia's characteristic lightness of touch, the fiction (which is etymologically, the "fashioning", from the Latin *fingere*, to shape) of historical fact.

Lucy Cavendish College, University of Cambridge

Works cited

Butterfield, Herbert *The Historical Novel* (Cambridge: Cambridge University Press 1924)

Firth, C.H. "Historical Novels" London, Historical Association Leaflet 51, 1922

Harman, Claire *Sylvia Townsend Warner-A Biography* (London: Chatto & Windus 1989

Maxwell, William (ed) *Letters: Sylvia Townsend Warner* (London: Chatto & Windus 1982)

Trevelyan, George Macaulay *The Present Position of History* (London: Longmans, Green and Co 1927)

Warner, George Townsend *A Brief Survey of British History, etc.* (London: Blackie & Son, Limited 1899)

_____. *Landmarks in British Industrial History* (London: Blackie & Son, Limited 1899)

Rickword, *et al*, "Sylvia Townsend Warner: A Celebration"; PNR 23 (1981)

Postgate, R.W. (ed) *Revolution from 1789 to 1906: Documents* (London:Grant Richards Ltd 1920)

Warner, George Townsend and CHK Marten *The Groundwork of British History* (London: Blackie & Son, Limited 1912)

_____. *Tillage, Trade and Invention* (London: Blackie & Son 1912)

Warner, Sylvia Townsend "A Love Match" in Tate, Trudi (ed) *Women, Men and the Great War: An Anthology of Stories* (Manchester: Manchester University press 1995).

_____. *Diaries* (edited by Claire Harman) (London: Chatto &Windus 1994)

_____. *Lolly Willowes* (London: Chatto & Windus 1926)

_____. *Mr Fortune's Maggot* (London: Chatto & Windus 1927)

_____. *Summer Will Show* (London: Chatto & Windus 1936)

_____. *The Corner That Held Them* (London: Chatto & Windus 1948)

_____. "The Historical Novel" in Stewart, Donald Ogden (ed) *Fighting Words* (New York: Harcourt Brace and Company 1940) pp49-52

Notes

[1] One such school's website announces that its "more able, keen historians" meet each week to prepare for the Townsend Warner History Prize. www.st-aubyns.brighton-hove.sch.uk/history.htm 29 January 2002.

[2] *The Harrovian*, vol xxix (1916) p96

[3] Warner, Sylvia Townsend "The Historical Novel" p50. "The Historical Novel" is a transcript of Warner's lecture to the Third Congress of the League of American Writers and appears in Stewart, Donald Ogden (ed) *Fighting Words* (New York: Harcourt Brace and Company 1940)

[4] See the description of Sylvia's childhood in Harman, Claire *Sylvia Townsend Warner-A Biography* (London: Chatto & Windus 1989) particularly, p20

[5] Excerpts from a note that Warner wrote retrospectively (during the 1960s) about the composition of *Summer Will Show* (1936). The note is included in Maxwell, William (ed) *Letters: Sylvia Townsend Warner* (London: Chatto & Windus 1982) p40

[6] Warner, George Townsend *Landmarks in British Industrial History* (London: Blackie & Son, Limited 1899) preface

[7] Warner, George Townsend and CHK Marten *The Groundwork of British History* (London: Blackie & Son, Limited 1912) p vi

[8] Warner, Sylvia Townsend *Diaries* (edited by Claire Harman) (London: Chatto & Windus 1994) p98

[9] Postgate, R.W. (ed) *Revolution from 1789 to 1906:documents* (London:Grant Richards Ltd 1920) pvii

[10] Warner, Sylvia Townsend "The Historical Novel" p50

[11] The tract that the heroine, Sophia Willoughby, begins to read at the end of the novel (and which the reader reads with her) reproduces the opening lines of the Communist Manifesto.

[12] Warner, George Townsend *A Brief Survey of British History, etc.* (London: Blackie & Son, Limited 1899) preface

[13] Warner, Sylvia Townsend "A Love Match" in Tate, Trudi (ed) *Women, Men and the great War: An Anthology of Stories* (Manchester: Manchester University Press 1995). The story's first publication was in 1961

[14] Butterfield, Herbert *The Historical Novel* (Cambridge: Cambridge University Press 1924). Butterfield recognises that "historians cry out because a ...[novelist] tampers with history (p6) but argues that fiction has a "peculiar virtue...as the gateway to the past" (preface) because "it helps our imagination to build up its idea of the past." (p2)

[15] Trevelyan, George Macaulay *The Present Position of History* (London: Longmans, Green and Co 1927) p28

[16] Trevelyan 1927 p9

[17] See, for example, Firth, C.H. "Historical Novels" London, Historical Association Leaflet 51, 1922. Firth notes that both "Board of Education and Army Education circulars" were recommending the use of historical novels. In the companion pamphlet on "Foreign Historical Novels" Harold Temperley observes that novelists such as Thackeray and Scott were not "composing real history" but, rather, "they filter its white light picturesquely through their gorgeous fancy." (p5)

[18] In this novel there is a complex network of symbolic puns : "Willowes" is the name of a family much concerned with its family tree; one which thinks of itself as dynastic and immemorial, as the "house of Willowes" (p9). It actually turns out to be the *contents* of the Willowes houses (especially the furniture and the books) that regulate the Willowes traditions, even though the Willowes homes are, themselves, regulated in "traditional" ways. Indeed, Warner even uses the family furniture to show how tradition is (literally) furnished. See Sykes, Rosemary "The Willowes Pattern" in *The Journal of the Sylvia Townsend Warner Society* 2001.

[19] Warner, Sylvia Townsend "The Historical Novel" pp50-51

[20] Warner, Sylvia Townsend *Lolly Willowes* 1926

[21] Warner, Sylvia Townsend "The Historical Novel"

[22] Diary entry for 17 March, 1941. See Harman, Claire (ed) *The Diaries of Sylvia Townsend Warner* (London: Chatto & Windus 1994)

[23] These possible titles are listed in notebook held in the Sylvia Townsend Warner and Valentine Ackland Archive, held at Dorset County Museum.

[24] In *The Corner That Held Them*, we are told that "in one house, every monk had died. In another, every monk but one." In *Tillage, Trade and Invention* George Townsend Warner states that "At the monastery of Heveringland,prior and canons died to a man; not one escaped. At Hickling, one canon survived." See Warner, George Townsend *Tillage, Trade and Invention*, (London: Blackie & Son 1912) , pp53-54

[25] Sylvia discussed the "Marxian" origins of her novel in "Sylvia Townsend Warner in Conversation", an interview included in the celebration of her life and work published in *PNR* 23 (1981).

[26] Page references are to the 1988 Virago Press edition.

CHAPTER 7

Sylvia Townsend Warner and the Historical Novel 1936-1948

Chris Hopkins

Sylvia Townsend Warner wrote three historical novels in the period from the mid-thirties to the end of the forties: *Summer Will Show* (1936), *After The Death of Don Juan* (1938), and *The Corner That Held Them* (1948). Each uses a strikingly different form in the possible repertoire of historical fiction types. This has usually (and in some senses rightly) been seen as a result of Townsend Warner's individual genius, of the difficulty of placing her work easily into pre-existing novel genres. However, there has been no previous attempt to trace her use of the historical novel across the period. The essay will explore the differences in form between the three historical fictions, as well as her critical comments in a lecture she gave on 'The Historical Novel' in 1939[1].

As Rosemary Sykes has noted in an interesting paper delivered at the Modern Language Association Convention 2003[2], Sylvia Townsend Warner was the daughter of a well-known historian and teacher, George Townsend Warner, who contributed to her keen engagement with education at home. Sykes points out that Sylvia had a sophisticated understanding of history and historiography, and that her uses of history may among other things critique her father's 'empiricist and imperialist'[3] sense of historical narrative:

> One of the ironies when considering the works of both father and daughter is that it was Sylvia (musicologist, creative writer) who handled original manuscripts as she carried out research for the Tudor Church Music Project, and near contemporary accounts as she researched her novels,

whilst her father (historian, purveyor of fact) admits that his skills lay in composition. . . .To return to the words of William Maxwell: 'if storytelling had not appealed to her more, Sylvia Townsend Warner might have been a formidable historian'. I suggest that she *was* a formidable historian, one whose understanding and use of story-telling reveals the fictiveness of any single, historical 'real'. In Sylvia's fiction we are shown, playfully, with Sylvia's characteristic lightness of touch, the fiction (which is etymologically, the 'fashioning', from the Latin *fingere*, to shape) of historical fact.[4]

Sykes particularly draws attention to *The Corner That Held Them* as a novel which refuses to offer a grand narrative of history. There is, I think, room to develop this insight further by exploring how this historical novel and its two predecessors reflect on history and narrative.

It has sometimes been forgotten that the historical novel was an extremely important political genre in England and Europe during the nineteen-thirties[5], possessing much potential for leftist writers to explore the dialectic of history in a realised and textured way. There were many writers on the left working in the genre, including Naomi Mitchison, and other less well remembered writers. There was also an associated theory of the historical novel, or at least of history and the novel [6] This body of theory can help us understand some of the meanings of the genre during the period. Thus there are discussions of how history relates to the representation of reality in books such as Ralph Fox's *The Novel and the People* (1937), Philip Henderson's *Literature* (1935) and his *The Novel Today* (1936). Lukacs' *The Historical Novel* of 1937 (though not available in English till 1962) is the most substantial and explicit critical discussion of the historical novel in the period: it has a number of parallels with the less exhaustive English treatments of the genre. There seem also to be parallels between Lukacs' understanding of the historical novel and elements of Sylvia's practice of the form. Pleasingly, there is also a record of a brief lecture of some one thousand words on 'The Historical Novel'[7] by Sylvia herself, where she reflects explicitly on the historical novel.

This seems a good place to start understanding Townsend Warner's engagement with the form before exploring the views of history within the novels themselves.

The lecture was given in 1939 at the Third Congress of the League of American Writers in New York. It was published by Harcourt Brace the following year in a book called *Fighting Words*, which adopted the curious procedure of loosely linking lectures by various writers together into 'chapters'. This happily preserves some of Sylvia's thoughts about the form as of 1939. The lecture starts with a recognition that the historical novel by the end of the nineteenth century was a traditional, even domesticated form, and also shows a thoughtful consideration of the devices of the genre: 'When I was young I read everything in the house, including historical novels, and two things struck me'. The two things are interesting formalist observations:

> First, that historical novels had usually long and frequent observations of scenery – I supposed in order that the author might have a spell of taking it easy. Oaks and brooks get along through the centuries without much fuss about being 'period'. Second that the period quality of the characters in these novels was a class distinction. The upper class characters were fully period. But the servants and the peasant and the social what-not had scarcely a period rag to cover them . . .They belonged to the date of the author.[8]

The first point though seemingly throw-away neatly brings out the need for historical novels to use broadly realist devices, some of which did not necessarily require much historical imagination. This introduces the more forceful second point, that historical portrayal in these novels has difficulties in periodising all of its aspects, and that these problems of representation surface through anachronistic representations of different social classes. In fact, according to Townsend Warner's observations, these versions of the historical novel cannot help but operate half in a period social world and half in a modern one. She suggests three possible reasons for this confused temporality:

First (and we can dismiss it forthwith) that the author wasn't going to bother with such small fry. He was too aristocratic. Second, that authors of historical novels are all near-Marxists, and were expressing the view that the closer you are to the bony structure, the hungrier you are and the harder you work, the more permanent are your class characteristics; or to put it another way, it is only the rich who can afford to be up to date, who can display strong period characteristics, whereas the poor can get along with the minimum of fashion.

The third reason which seems to me the likeliest, is this: if you examine the historical novel you will find that it is the working-class characters who fill the role of the commentator, the analyst, the person who sums things up. The noble sentiments, the villainous sentiments, go into the mouths of the ruling characters; but when it comes to a piece of plain common sense, it is the ruled who speak. So I would suggest that the authors kept their working-class characters contemporary because of this structural function of pinning the story together by comment and analysis . . . these commenting characters were kept contemporary because writers felt it the safest way in keeping them life-like.(pp. 50-1)

It is interesting to see the first explanation immediately dismissed: it seems at least conceivable from a leftist point of view that if the historical novelist is from a dominant class, he/she might indeed be mainly or at least apparently concerned with the equivalent dominant classes in the period in which the novel is set. But Townsend Warner starts from the assumption stated in a previous paragraph that: 'you will agree with me that in almost every piece of historical fiction it is the characters of the ruled that come bursting out of the texture' (p.50). Thus, it seems unlikely to her that 'the ruled' are contemporary merely due to lack of authorial attention. Her second explanation takes almost an opposite view of how author-class and character-class interact: whatever the historical novelist's own class position, they will, perhaps unconsciously, recognise the underlying and relatively unchanging reality given to the workers by their economic position. The second argument may suggest among other things how strong the association is in Sylvia Townsend Warner's mind between Marxism and the form of the historical novel. Nevertheless, this political explanation is rejected in favour of a third which is more a matter of narrative structure: such novels need a commentator who mediates the meaning of events for the reader, and the most meaningful interpretation comes from characters who have the 'life-like' aspect given them by being of the reader's own period. This sense that the past must be interpreted through and for the present is in itself an historiographical understanding, leading Sylvia Townsend Warner here to a quasi-postmodern conception of 'the impossibility of history', of understanding the past in its own terms. This is not her final view, as we shall see, for this is partially an aspect of her critique of this kind of historical novel.

There is a similarity between the second and third explanations of the temporal/class problem – in which the common woman or man is the most reliable guide to 'truth'. Indeed, if this point about differential periodisation of social classes begins as a criticism of a type of novel, it also to an extent develops as an insight into a central but problematic device of the historical novel. Townsend Warner's next observation about the contemporary historical novel develops further the importance of the relationship in the genre between past and present, noting a different but perhaps even more flawed approach to the representation of the past:

> All this, of course, applies to the traditional historical novel. More recently there has been a revolt against this, and *all* the characters in historical novels are of the present day, contemporary in speech, in behaviour, in motive, in psychology. But the talisman is not infallible, and these characters straight out of modern life may make up a perfectly lifeless book. (p.51-2)

This implies that certain fashions of periodising characters have fallen out of favour because they lead to an uneven stylistic texture and to characters who lack conviction. Therefore, contemporary novelists have tried to give the life that was previously only bestowed on 'the ruled' to all their characters by giving them each a contemporary feel. But this must destroy the interpretative function of the 'working–class' characters, so that there is no longer the partly productive tension of the past being viewed through the present, of formerly dominant ideologies (it might be chivalry, for example) being exposed to the critique of modern 'common sense'. Such novels have arrived at a deep misunderstanding of the form: 'there must, it seems, be some recognition of history in the historical novel. The writer of the historical novel cannot escape the obligation of a period' (p.52).

Sylvia Townsend Warner then moves onto a combined explanation of what the historical novel should do and an observation that the contemporary leftist historical novel is not always free of the fault of making everything modern:

> In all ages, the prime motives are the same; fear, love, anger, hunger, necessity, ambition – the old gang. Nor has the economic structure altered that much. To get some work to get enough to eat to get some work . . . And the reactions to the economic structure are pretty constant too, but constant with a qualification. There were strong men before Agememnon. There were tolerable Marxists before Marx. But they were before Marx. And an historical novelist who includes (and I think the historical novelist should) the economic ground-base, must simultaneously recognize the social-economic variations which move above that ground-base. Thomas More and Latimer, for instance, wrote as socialists; but they were Christian socialists. Oliver Cromwell had the career of a fascist leader; but he was a fascist before imperialism. (p. 52)

This partly restates a point which Marx made, and which Lukacs quotes: 'One can understand tribute and tithe etc. when one knows about ground rent, one must not, however, identify them'.[9] Sylvia Townsend Warner sees the historical novelist's function as having a broadly humanist element in the sense that there are aspects of human identity which remain understandable across the ages, but that they must also represent the particular truth of how lives were realised under the different economic organisation of the past:

> Human nature does not change etc., but human thinking alters a great deal, is conditioned by what it has been taught, what it believes, or disbelieves; what it admires in art or nature; at what age it marries; to what extent it has

outwitted weather (it was the medieval winters, cold, dark and boring, that taught the troubadours to praise the spring); what careers are open to it; whether it reads Aristotle or Plato; whether it believes in witches or planets. (p.53)

Clearly this is a Marxist approach to the historical novel: as the idea of 'social being' producing 'consciousness', and the explicit reference to the base / superstructure explanation show (though the latter is ingeniously shifted a little into a different discourse by Sylvia's use of the musical terms 'ground(-base)' and 'variations', suggesting her subtle sense of the interplay between the two[10]). It is this nuanced and properly historicist approach grounded in Marxist thought which Sylvia sees as producing the truest kind of historical novel. She is still though very wary of falsifying the relationship between the past and the present, as she warns against the practice of understanding the past through contemporary understandings, without seeing that the identity of roles across time is structural rather than exact: Sir Thomas More can usefully be seen as a kind of socialist in terms of his attitude to the oppressed, but he cannot accurately be depicted as a modern socialist. Novels set before the nineteenth or twentieth century period may have socialist-like or fascistic figures, but there must remain an element of analogy. Indeed, the earlier sense in the lecture of the partial benefits of a disjunction between past and present in historical representation is still implicitly here in this final section of the argument. There have to be acts of bridging time which do not wholly efface themselves, do not forget that interpretation is always involved. Thus, as in all historical study, the understanding of the past through novels is always an attempt rather than an empiricist success:

> If you know these things ['what it believes or disbelieves' et seq], then you may have a chance of knowing *all* your characters, that is to say, a chance of making them life-like, or bringing the whole of your book to life. (p.53)[11]

The lecture is an intriguing insight into Sylvia Townsend Warner's thinking about the historical novel at the end of the thirties, and it concentrates clearly on different possibilities within the genre; however, one thing it does not do is directly to explain the variety of her own practice, already quite sharply instanced in the differences between *Summer Will Show* and *After the Death of Don Juan*. The clear recommendations at the end of the lecture are about general principles rather than specific forms: the good historical novel should be based on 'a little research', but should not be too dominated by excessive antiquarian accuracy ('it is sometimes better not to haunt museums', p.53). However, as we shall see, many of the issues raised about form in the lecture are indeed engaged with in the three novels also.

Summer Will Show seems to belong to a nineteenth-century novel tradition in many respects. It is a panoramic portrayal of a particular city, showing the full range of social classes, maintaining an ability to show how the exterior reality and the interior reality of characters' thoughts are interdependent. It is strongly realist with much attention paid to the careful depiction of a material world:

> Some tin coffee-pots, long wands of golden bread, a sausage in a paper chemise, gave a domesticated appearance to the barricade, as though the objects had arrived of their own good will in order to assure the beds and tables that there was nothing after all, so particularly odd or discreditable in having spent a night in the street.[12]

It thus fulfils the essentially realist characteristic of the historical novel as identified by Richard Maxwell: 'Historical fiction is by definition referential, gesturing toward a world commonly understood to have existed'.[13] The novel also falls in with Lukacs' idea that there is a close kinship between the classic realist novel and the 'authentic' use of the historical novel form, as exemplified for him by Balzac's histories of the immediate past and the present.[14] In short *Summer Will Show* adopts in many ways a nineteenth-century form of a kind which is in fact contemporaneous to its setting. Some critical comments on the novel perhaps do not draw much attention to the form precisely for this reason: the novel is using what are recognisably 'normal' novel conventions, emphasising mimesis and the reader's engagement with the narrative. Thus Claire Harman comments on the novel's effect:

> The ordinariness of historical events, even revolutions, is conveyed intact: there is not a breath of quaintness or 'period feel' to the writing. As in her later novels, there is a complete identification with the period chosen, a contemporary feel which goes beyond historical accuracy to a sense of historical actuality.[15]

And Barbara Brothers similarly observes a conventional novelistic sense of social reality represented with all its texture: 'Warner's novel sheds light upon the relationship between the individual and society, reflecting individuals as both constituted and constricted by social values and customs'[16] This is not to say that there is nothing new in the novel's use of these conventions, as critics like Terry Castle and Thomas Foster have suggested:

> In *Summer Will Show* no one story is allowed to achieve either completion or complete authority; no narrative perspective is privileged over all others. Warner thereby deploys the modernist technique of 'transforming interruption . . . into a deliberate strategy as a sign of women's writing' that Jane Marcus locates in Virginia Woolf's experiments with narrative form'.[17]

Christina Rauch extends Foster's argument suggesting widespread subversion of existing conventions in Townsend Warner's work despite its apparent continuity with previous fictional forms:

> Warner's novels at first glance fit in perfectly with the familiar narrative traditions of the eighteenth and nineteenth centuries. . . However an unsettling indeterminacy or unreliability emerges from Warner's fiction, which silently subverts prominent conventions of what we could call the traditional narrative discourse, and effectively places her work within the

> context of Modernist literature. . . Narrative authority in the text is dispersed among the characters themselves as well as between the narrator and the characters [so that] no reliable statement about Minna Lemuel seems possible. . .Warner here maintains that individual narratives cannot contain the complexity of reality: each new story about Minna always produces a new and different version of her, which may give its recipient some new, but never more, knowledge.[18]

This emphasis on interpretability in Warner's novels chimes well with the points made above about the central place of interpretation in her sense of historiography.[19]

There is then a general critical consensus that *Summer Will Show* partakes of nineteenth-century traditions, while also breaking new ground. Gillian Beer suggests that one of the characteristics of Townsend Warner's work is that it even subverts itself: 'Her narratives never rest content with their initial project.'[20] One feature of *Summer Will Show* which has not been noticed is that it does indeed contain an internal critique of certain aspects of the historical novel form and which can be linked to some of the issues Sylvia later raised about historical novels in her lecture. Though, as we have seen, the novel has been praised for its lack of 'quaintness or "period feel" ' there is actually an intriguing vein of the quaint or antique in the novel, which is linked to ideas of the literary and the histrionic. What are we to make of Wlodimir MacGusty?:

> 'Min-na!' exclaimed Macgusty, bounding acrosss the room between one syllable and the next, throwing down his hat and falling on one knee beside the pink sofa. 'Minna! Unfortunate child, what distresses you? What catastrophe is this? Why do you weep? (p.316)

Clearly he is a ludicrous figure, with his melodramatic behaviour and his peculiar speech, constantly exclamatory and rhetorical. It is clear that this is Macgusty's own quaintness, but it does break the novel's general approach to speech. Macgusty's speech and manners are evidently not contemporary, and he is surely an allusion to a romantic dramatic aspect of the nineteenth-century historical novel.

Close links are suggested between the historical novel and the romantic revolutionary when Ingelbrecht reads out to Minna and Sophia his critique of such figures:

> *There are some revolutionaries . . . who seem incapable of feeling a durable anger against the conditions which they seek to overthrow. . . . The anger which they undoubtedly feel is neutralised by the pleasure they experience in expressing it .. . when they have finished their speech or poignarded their tyrant, they are in such a state of satisfied excitement that they are almost ready to forgive the state of society which allows them such abuses on which to avenge themselves . . .*
>
> *In using that antiquated and romantic expression, 'poignarded the tyrant,' I use it with intention. These revolutionaries are penetrated with artistic and historical feeling, they turn naturally to the weapons of the past, and to methods which, by being outmoded, appear to be chivalrous (I point out that there must be an element of the gothic in all chivalry. No perfectly contemporary action can be described as chivalrous). This tendency . . . is abetted by another characteristic proper to persons of this temperament – great technical facility. The argument that it is easier to kill a man with a gun than with a rapier carries little force with them, because they are already so skilful with a rapier . ..* (pp. 268-70)[21]

It seems that here a witty parallel is drawn between the characteristics of romantic revolutionaries and of a certain historical novel tradition. Both turn to the archaic language and the ' weapons of the past'. Both show 'great technical facility' so that they are in a way able to engage deeply with the past, since they are already in command of the 'outmoded' conventions of a past age: 'they are already so skilful with the rapier'. But that engagement with history is a falsified one, 'chivalrous', rather than contemporary. Indeed, the appeal of such figures / novels is in their 'chivalry'. As 'No perfectly contemporary action can be described as chivalrous', these figures / novels appeal to an audience which enjoys the emotion they generate exactly because it does not ask them to make any systematic connection to the contemporary world. This version of the revolutionary / the historical novel is 'penetrated with artistic and historical feeling', but actually has no historical perspective, because it does not link the immediate action with any longer term view of history. Just as in Lukacs's view, certain forms of historical novel are merely fossilised forms, antiquarian impostures of a real engagement with history, so too in Ingelbrecht's analysis certain forms of revolutionary activity are not actually revolutionary. Or as Townsend Warner puts it in her lecture, such figures / novels are despite their 'noble sentiments' in a deeper sense 'lifeless' (p. 51).

This meditation on the historical novel is striking in itself in giving us an intratextual discussion of the form, but even more importantly it is a key to one of the novel's central concerns. The phrase 'gusts of eloquence' (p. 270) may suggest the link to Mcgusty, but he is not the only character for whom Ingelbrecht's analysis provides insight. The much more sinister Gaston is surely such another 'spectacular' figure:

> 'Begun!' It is in full flow, nothing can stop it now. Paris is ours! . . . Tomorrow night there will be bloodshed . . . One must have the night . . . one must have the effect of torchlight, the Rembrandtesque shadows, the solemnity and uncertainty of darkness, Besides, feelings run higher at night and there are more people at leisure to become spectators' (p. 148)

Gaston's speech has some similarity to Mcgusty's, and there is much theatrical reference. Where Mcgusty is a sentimentalist, Gaston is without concern for individuals; what matters is that his show must go off well, that there be the bloodshed for which he has planned: 'children are essential for the right feeling, and I have arranged for the children' (p. 149).

Mcgusty and Gaston are relatively minor characters, but another highly theatrical figure is not: Minna herself. When Ingelbrecht is analysing romantic revolutionaries, Minna makes a significant response: ' "If I could kill one tyrant," murmured Minna, "I would die happy." ' (p.269). This is, of course, to confess to having an affinity with this type of romantic revolutionary herself. However, there is a perhaps an opposition in this novel between an absolute truth – of which Ingelbrecht and Martin are the spokesmen, – and the seductive illusions of theatre and storytelling. When Ingelbrecht leaves the house, Minna articulates this very clearly:

> 'I do, I do appreciate him!' exclaimed Minna. 'I appreciate him implicitly. If he were to say to me, Minna, never another word, no more stories of the oppressed, no more of your sorceries with fairy-tales, I would sew up my mouth. But this afternoon how could I help feeling a little dulled? . . . saying to myself – that Sophia . . . will she ever come back? (p.273)

Summer Will Show reworks the nineteenth-century social and historical novel forms in order to produce a conversion narrative of a kind produced by other thirties' writers. It has been suggested that the political narrative is not entirely integrated:

> The book is not properly a propaganda effort. It was started long before Sylvia espoused Communism. Because she did not discard the earlier part, the political message of the book is not completely integrated in the way one would expect of a novel written primarily to promote the Party.[22]

This seems a slightly crude view of what a 'Party' novel had to be like in the thirties, but perhaps also the observation misses something of how subtle the novel is. If aspects of the earlier part of Sophia's story were written before the political centre of the novel was established, this may nevertheless contribute to the sense of a real change of conviction on her part. And in fact the novel is not about simply joining a political party who have obvious command of the truth. Sophia meets a range of revolutionaries and is able through moving in a much wider social environment to see that much of what she once held to be self-evident was, rather, class-prejudice and ideology. The novel is centrally concerned with the stripping away of illusions, but these are not the monopoly of the reactionary. Indeed, it is notably interested in how bound up the revolution is with a variety of kinds of illusionism. It may well be that there is a real ambivalence in the novel about how storytelling relates to Marxism's objective understanding of history. Possibly Townsend Warner's sense of the complexity and inevitable partiality of historiography runs into some tension here with her discovery of a clearly defined Marxist historical grand narrative?

All accounts agree that Sylvia Townsend Warner's fifth novel, *After the Death of Don Juan*, had a subdued impact in 1938: 'got very little attention of any sort'[23]. Though there has been some discussion of the novel, it has still not received anything like the discussion devoted to *Summer Will Show*. In her interesting essay already referred to above, Christina Rauch suggests that 'we could say of the ideal reader of Sylvia Townsend Warner's novels that she or he must possess an inexhaustible capacity for riddle solving'[24]. Since Sylvia famously said of *After the Death of Don Juan* that it was **'a parable or an allegory, or what you will**, of the political chemistry of the Spanish War'[25], we should expect there to be a substantial degree of riddle solving involved in reading this novel. We should also expect, from the suggestive phrase 'political chemistry', a sophisticated approach to the representation of Spain.

There has not been a concerted attempt to read the 'parable' at the rich level of detail and sophistication which the narrative can sustain. It is clear that while *After the Death of Don Juan* is an historical novel, it is one of a very different form from *Summer Will Show*. Though there are certainly elements of the 'parable' in the earlier novel, it could also be read as a realist historical novel. Moreover, *After the Death of Don Juan* has a mythical status as an evident and ironic re-telling of a story already known to the reader. This makes it very unlike the predominant realist mode of its predecessor. The ironic readings suggested for minor characters such as Mcgusty and Gaston have now moved closer to the apparent centre stage: 'It was expected that Don Ottavia, Dona Ana's betrothed, would avenge the commander's death; or at any rate attempt to: Don Juan was a practised swordsman. Dona Ana, however, declared that vengeance must be the business of heaven'.[26] Rather than being invited to empathise with characters' own viewpoints of themselves, we are here held at a distance, invited to see that the given motives are not the real motives. Dona Ana, as she does throughout, uses the language of religion to pursue more earthly desires. The characters manipulate codes for their own purposes. These distancing effects are mainly reserved for the aristocratic characters; they are, in the terms identified in Sylvia's lecture, the noble but relatively lifeless characters, who deploy formal and apparently heroic discourses. Thus Don Ottavio uses the language of courtly love, while Dona Ana uses the language of piety, both of which register as archaic: ' I live to serve you' (p.2), 'Have I lived . . .to be called impious? And by a layman? (p.7). Sometimes, the formal language and motives slip, as when Don Ottavio protests against Dona Ana's second obligation: 'It would be throwing away money, I mean it would be flying in the face of Providence, to have masses said for the repose of his soul'. (p.6). This never happens to Dona Ana, however, who maintains her theatrical religious posture at all times, never admitting to any but the most proper motives: 'When next he saw her she was in a different mood, rigidly exalted, bearing herself like a figure in a tragedy . ."Avenge him!" she exclaimed (p.13). This combination of slippage and lack of understanding on Don Ottavio's part and of a mask-like performance on Dona Ana's reinforces the sense that the characters from this elite class live in a welter of contradictions, both conscious and unrecognised. The peasants, however, do seem much more realistically portrayed and thus, again in Sylvia's lecture terms, are more contemporary-sounding (or, anyway, to use her rejected explanation, 'closer ... to the bony structure'): ' "Is he dead, is he off our backs at last? . . . We have land, and we work it, and by rights we should be making every year a little money to put by" '. (p.108-9)

This social differentiation by periodisation is not the ideal historical novel which the lecture finally suggests, but it does seem to have some explanatory power for how *After the Death of Don Juan* works. The parable nature of the novel also clearly raises a problem which the lecture discusses, that of confusing historical analogy with historical identity ('Oliver Cromwell had the career of a fascist leader; but he was a fascist before imperialism'). Don Juan might appear to be a similar case. At least one critic has taken the view that Townsend Warner's historical novels are essentially about the present and not the past; Barbara Brothers states that in *Summer Will Show* Warner uses 'the historical novel as a vehicle for contemporary commentary and criticism just as some writers of science fiction use future worlds to illuminate the present'.[27]

Brothers takes a similar approach to *After the Death of Don Juan* giving a very specific account of the novel's parable.[28] She argues that the allegory specifically refers to the condition of the Spanish Republic in 1931, and that the novel traces the beginnings of the Spanish Civil War from that period. I do not disagree with the general tenor of these insights, but the straightforward one-to-one mapping between eighteenth-century Spain and Spain 1931 to 1936 sits slightly uneasily with the critical view that Sylvia Townsend Warner's novels are subtle and 'riddling', and also runs counter to her concern not to fall into such literal historical translations. I think there is another level of historicisation that can broaden our understanding of how this novel works, and which was very familiar to leftist intellectuals in the thirties.

The tradition of the historical novel and the allegory as political forms in the thirties is rooted in a sense of the explanatory power of broad historical frameworks. History, and historical novels, could help to understand the politics of the present because that present arose from the past, and because there was a pattern to history which meant that valid parallels could be drawn between different periods. In this dual view of history: the past exists both for itself and as a 'type' of another period in the present. This mode of thinking worried Lukacs in his study *The Historical Novel* (1937), because he feared that in crude instances the parallels drawn distorted the specificity of each period involved in the comparison

The direct and conceptual relationship with the present which prevails today reveals an immanent tendency to turn the past into a parable of the present, to wrest directly from history a 'fabula docet', and this conflicts with the real historical concreteness of the content . . .[suggesting] a direct, abstract and therefore unhistorical, merely allegorical relationship with the present.[29]

In the main *After the Death of Don Juan* does not invite this charge of simplification of past and present, though there are issues about the accuracy of parallels. The novel makes considerable efforts to tell a dual history, in which the two histories remain separate. It represents the lives of the peasants as concretely as possible as they might have been in eighteenth century Spain: it does not in a simple sense make them into twentieth-century workers, though it does make it easier for us to take their voices seriously. Equally, Don Saturno while evidently providing a parallel to modern liberalism can reasonably represent a Spanish aristocrat of the period who, though very much part of a feudal society, has an interest in Enlightenment rationalism. Perhaps the one striking exception is the figure of Don Juan. Though profligate sons were doubtless a real historical possibility in the eighteenth century, maybe his obvious prefiguring of fascism does give him a too immediate relationship with the present. It might be that his mythical status for much of the novel makes it more difficult to situate him in eighteenth century Spain as a type of a developing social class – and indeed his monstrous exceptionalism may seem particularly appropriate to the rise of fascism. Having argued that we need to remember a thirties tradition of reading historical novels as a form of parable, I can suggest how this set of ideas deepens our understanding of *After the Death of Don Juan*. To start with Don Saturno; he is usually identified as a would-be reformer. His failure to achieve is demonstrated by numerous accounts of his plans, including his own: 'To irrigate Tenorio Viejo has been for many years one of my dearest projects, Indeed, one may say that in Spain all water is in a sense holy water . . .. The rapid shift from description of the intention to an aesthetic generalisation is characteristic. For the people of Tenorio Viejo, irrigation is the key issue for all their livelihoods, and some, at times, almost believe that Don Saturno will deliver. But many are sceptical, as we see in the conversation in the inn, where the reported death of Don Juan is immediately linked to the hope of irrigation: 'Always promise, never perform'(p.116). The acute analysis here – that Don Saturno's strength is in linguistic gestures rather than fulfilment of them – is in line with Marx and Engels's critique of the limitations of previous philosophies: they could describe the world, but not change it. Don Saturno is very much an Enlightenment philosopher: he knows about many areas of human knowledge, including science, economics,[30] and history. But he cannot apply his knowledge. Indeed, often, his knowledge allows him to evade the present, as when he tries to divert Don Juan from too specific an interest in irrigation:

> Don Saturno began to speak of the value of irrigation, irrigation in general. He quoted figure to prove how with a steady water supply the land would give a greater yield, in some cases two harvests instead of one . . . He sketched arguments for supposing the aquaduct of Segovia to be of Roman construction . . . He talked for some time and did not once refer to the irrigation of Tenorio Viejo (p.241).

In this instance the evasion is ultimately a failure – unfortunately revealing an even more profound incapacity to understand and deal with the dangers of the present in the form of his son Don Juan.

Don Saturno focuses not only a critique of Enlightenment thought, but a common thirties critique of liberalism, that it could understand progressive ideas, but never translate them into reality. The passage also concisely makes the point that, for liberalism, cultural knowledge has become a way of reinforcing illusion rather than unmasking it. Nevertheless, even at the end of the novel, it is clear that Don Saturno has no sympathy for Don Juan's violent solutions to Tenorio Viejo's problems. As Wendy Mulford so accurately puts it:

> Objectively, each character, even the sceptical and reforming Don Saturno, is bound into one interest or the other – in the Don's case, literally, as Juan ties him to a chair to prevent him warning the peasants of their betrayal.[31]

Our understanding of Don Juan himself can also be deepened by a similar sense of thirties critical discourses about history and parables. Don Saturno is surprised when his returned son shows interest in his ideas about irrigation. But in fact Don Juan is precisely not interested in the idea, but in the facts of irrigation: ' "I can't be interested in the past", said Don Juan. "I want to know why you don't irrigate this place. Surely it would be very profitable?" ' (p. 241). Don Saturno is at first pleased, thinking that Don Juan will one day come to share his 'tastes' (p. 242). But this is exactly the wrong word, for Don Juan has no time for the aesthetic: his interests are in results. The son of Don Saturno will bring the action of which his father was incapable, but his radicalism is not that for which most people in Tenorio Viejo wished. Though Don Juan is usually read as a figure of fascism, the dual history of the novel can see him in two ways. In contemporary thirties terms he is a figuring of fascism, with his urge for violent action and for coercive exploitation. However, in relation to the eighteenth century, he may also be seen as a figure of the new attitudes of capitalism: 'it seems to me that in five year's time, there would be a twenty per cent profit' (p.242). This makes sense in terms of thirties thought about the relationship between capitalism and fascism, in which fascism was seen as the most naked form of capitalism, its logical descendant, under which the ideological masks of liberalism had given way to more brutally explicit forms of power relations.

After the Death of Don Juan, in short, like *Summer Will Show* shows a very acute sense of the possibilities of the historical novel form and of contemporary debates about history and the novel. Her next historical novel, published some twelve years later, *The Corner That Held Them* (1948) explores yet another version of the historical novel. In her introduction to the Virago edition, Claire Harman observes that:

> Anyone could be forgiven, when reading the first few pages of *The Corner That Held Them*, for thinking that they had picked up a historical novel. The opening episode, brightened by passions and the colour of blood, is certainly in that tradition, but as the book progresses, the reader becomes aware that it is poised ambiguously between a history and a fiction, for *The Corner That Held Them* is a masterly pieceof contrived realism. . . There is no quaint language and no scene-painting.[32]

Of course, I do think that *The Corner That Held Them* is an historical novel, and equally it can be said that the two previous novels also avoided quaint language and scene painting, except for specific purposes as discussed above. Nevertheless, the comment brings out well how far this is from the parable form of *After The Death of Don Juan*. We seem to be returning to, or exceeding, the realism of *Summer Will Show*, without even the odd 'antiquarian' character like Mcgusty. Moreover, the classic novel form is not used here. Indeed, Townsend Warner noted this in a letter quoted by Harman: 'I still incline to call it People growing Old. It has no conversations and no pictures, it has no plot, and the characters are innumerable and insignificant'. There are some conversations, in fact, but it is true that much of the narrative is more concerned with characters' thoughts, and there is no conventional plot (indeed the novel just stops).[33] There are a large number of characters during the forty-year historical span of the novel, some of whom make brief appearances, others more extended ones. Broadly, one might say, as Claire Harman does[34] that the form is that of a chronicle: event follows event, but not all events are related by plot, and sometimes there is a lack of explanation of cause and effect. However, interestingly there is only one early portion of the narrative which is strictly in chronicle form:

> In 1208 came the Interdict.
> In 1223 lightning set fire to the granary.
> In 1257 the old reed and timber cloisters fell to bits in a gale . . .
> In 1270 there were disastrous floods, and this happened again seven years later. In 1238 hornets built in the brewhouse roof and the cellaress was stung in the lip and died. . . .

In 1332 a nun broke her vow and left the convent for a lover (p.11).

This early passage seems to have the function of signalling that the novel is chronicle-like and is thus liberated from having to be a strictly-connected narrative (or even grand narrative), but it also shows that local narratives have a constant tendency to develop within such an open form. Thereafter, themes do develop, are followed until their protagonists die or until another story becomes dominant in the life of the nunnery.

It is notable that in this historical novel which is liberated from a modern sense of history as explanation, characters, and even the narrator, often do explicitly speculate about history (more so than in the previous two historical novels). Soon after the foundation of the nunnery, the narrative voice comments on what the proper relationship of the nuns to history should be, and what it is:

> A good convent should have no history. Its life is hid with Christ who is above. History is of the world, costly and deadly, and the events it records usually deplorable: the year when the roof caught fire, the year of the summer flood . . . the year when Dame Dionysia had a baby by the bishop's clerk. Yet the events of history carry a certain exhilaration with them. Decisions are made, money is spent, strangers arrive, familiar characters appear in a new light, transfigured with unexpected goodness or badness. Few calamities fall on a religious house which are not at some time or other looked back upon with wistful regret. . . Men with their inexhaustible interest in themselves may do well enough in a wilderness, but the shallower egoism of women demands some nourishment from the outer world. (p.7-8).

Convents should have no history because they are concerned only with divine history which is outside time in the earthly sense. But that is an ideal, and in fact, the nuns are glad it is so. For it is notable that history as described here is though partly about fact is also largely about what can be done with those 'facts', about history as story. Thus even calamities can be recalled with a certain pleasure, 'a wistful regret', and perhaps even as it happens history gives narrative interest to the community's life, for villains turn out to be heroes and heroes to be villains.

Actually, the first prioress's sense that women need this kind of 'history' more than men may not be borne out by the rest of the novel. When the nun's priest Sir Ralph visits the villagers he finds that the men there seem to find history just as entertaining:

> Jesse and William then resumed their sober, untiring arguments . . . sometimes about events that had happened during the time of the Danes. It was an everlasting dispute how far the Danes had travelled up the Waxle stream. As far as Kitts Bend asserted William. Farther by a mile, Jesse maintained . . . where the ghost of Red Thane's daughter walked to this day.(p.83)

The narrative constantly returns to the central importance of stories, whether remotely plausible or not. Thus Dame Sibilla 'brought what to the bulk of the convent was almost as good as a dowry: a narrative' and 'whether one believed her stories' about flying hogs and friars who ascended into heaven, 'such stories were pleasant to listen to' (p.195). Henry Yellowlees, the custos of the nunnery returning from a failed mission to try to ensure that the nunnery receives a rent which they think they are owed, explicitly thinks about why there is no single version of reality:

> His fruitless errand which had been to the monks of Killdew a story for diner, and to himself a nut to crack, like a problem in mathematics, would be to the ladies of Oby a matter of bread and bacon. For each one of us lives in a microcosm, the solidity of this world is a mere game of mirrors, there can be no absolute existence for what is apprehended differently by all. And if he could have brought back the music-books his fruitless errand would have been for him as a return from the lands of Saba (p.215).

The reference to *ars nova* is significant, for this form of music, new in the fourteenth century as Sylvia Townsend Warner well knew, was distinguished

139

among other features by its use of multiple independent voices, or polyphony, which parallels Henry Yellowlees thoughts about the nature of reality and story[35]. It may also be significant that *ars nova* used metre differently from the preceding *ars antiqua*, commonly using duple instead of triple time and allowing different parts to move in different metres – perhaps an equivalent to the individual modernist experiences of time which a number of the novel's characters refer to.

Indeed, there seems no doubt that paradoxically the use of the 'primitive' chronicle form has a modernist aspect to it in this novel, emphasising that life does not progress in a conventionally plotted form, and that truth, time and experience are relative and flowing. Near the beginning of the essay I noted Rosemary Sykes's observation that the novel's use of the Waxle stream is used in opposition to her father's sense of British history's progressive stream. To this idea can be added a conscious play on the modernist idea of stream of consciousness, as when we see the nun's priest Sir Ralph thinking through how his thought-processes work:

> His thoughts, running with unusual lucidity . . . were like a transparent stream. They ran by, and by; and beneath them, like the river bed were the facts. . . But between him and the facts ran this glassy process of thinking, this flow of apprehending how it had all come about. (p.25)

Lukacs disaproved of the use of the chronicle form for historical fiction and of modernism precisely because neither in his view linked cause and effect in an adequate way and gave a totalising view of social development. However, for Townsend Warner, the chronicle / modernist form was clearly liberating and she saw no contradiction with her communist commitment, saying that the novel was started 'on the purest Marxian principles, because I was convinced that if you were going to give an accurate picture of the monastic life, you'd have to put in all their finances; how they made their money, how they dodged about from one thing to another and how very precarious it all was'.[36] Perhaps the preoccupation of the characters with their finances *and* with their thoughts and stories is a version of Sylvia's earlier idea in her historical novel lecture about how the historical novelist must take account of the social-economic variations which move above [the] ground-base', or of Sir Ralph's reflections on how thought relates to facts. In many ways, this novel explores possibilities which are not covered in Sylvia's historical novel lecture, but perhaps it does achieve her ideal of realising all the characters fully in their own right and without any 'contemporary' or mediating characters.

When I began this essay I thought that I might be able to historicise Sylvia Townsend's use of different forms of the historical novel over a period of just over a decade in terms of the impact of the political history unfolding during the nineteen thirties and forties. In fact, it has been more productive to trace a more literary-historical path through how she developed different forms of the historical novel. These developments are in some ways closely linked to debates about history and the novel in the thirties, since they clearly show a sophisticated engagement with contemporary debates about this relationship. However, I am not sure that there is a clear linear development which keeps pace with the 'external' history of the period, though it may be significant that there is a rejection of grand narrative after the second world war. What there does seem to be is a clear tension throughout the three novels between history as publicly agreed 'fact' and history as individually experienced, often through the form of myth or story. *Summer Will Show* perhaps comes closest at its conclusion to a sense that there is a single true history which can be grasped (though the importance of Minna's storytelling in changing Sophia's life is hardly overpowered), while *After the Death of Don Juan,* with more faith in the power of stories for good and bad, leaves the dying peasant rebels at its end hoping that one day their interrupted story will be more happily concluded. *The Corner That Held Them*, while historically extremely knowledgeable is the most evidently modernist in form, explicitly putting in fourteenth-century terms a number of modernist conceptions of how life is experienced. Perhaps what runs through each of the novels is a tension (and a productive one) between a feminine modernist sense of the multiplicity of explanation and interpretation and an engagement with a Marxist history which does have a grand narrative, if one capable of nuanced application. Above all though there is Sylvia Townsend Warner's command of the forms of the historical novel and of the impact these have on ideas of history. Gillian Beer notes that Townsend Warner's work seems prophetic of future developments in the novel:

> Perhaps the thing that now most stands out about her novelistic career in terms of genre is its prescience. If *After The Death of Don Juan* had been published not in 1936 but fifty years later, it would have been greeted as a magic-realist fiction . . .while *Summer Will Show* would be seen as part of the current vogue for novels that rewrite the nineteenth-century and the medieval *The Corner That Held Them* as a follower of Umberto Eco. But Warner in fact wrote each of these very diverse novels long before these critical templates were in place. She composed with an exploratory verve which is quite extraordinary.[37]

In fact, though, these proto-postmodern resonances, long before the contemporary critical exploration of 'historiographical metafiction' stem from Sylvia's sense of the complexity of history and of the possibilities of historical fiction, from sophisticated contemporary debates about these, and above all from an ability to explore in her fiction the impacts of different kinds of storytelling.

Sheffield Hallam University

Notes
[1] The lecture has not previously been discussed by critics, with the exception of Rosemary Sykes. I was unaware of it when I wrote my article on Sylvia Townsend Warner in 1995 (see end-note 5) and I am very grateful to Rosemary for bringing it to my attention in her paper referred to below in end-note 2.

[2] In a paper called ' "This was a Lesson in History": Sylvia Townsend Warner, George Warner and the Matter of History' part of the 'Sylvia Townsend Warner and the Currency of History' panel, organised by Connie Mason and Jennifer Poulos Nesbitt, San Diego, December 2003. I am very grateful to Rosemary Sykes for permission to quote from her paper before its publication: my essay draws on her insights and scholarly knowledge.

[3] Sykes, p.3

[4] Sykes pp. 1-2 and p. 11-12.

[5] See my article 'Sylvia Townsend Warner and the Marxist Historical Novel', *Literature and History*, Third Series, Vol.4.1, Spring 1995

[6] Lukacs identified in this vein Balzac as writing a kind of historical novel of the present: 'a consciously historical conception of the present' in *The Historical Novel*, English translation, 1962, Merlin Press, London, p. 92.

[7] The lecture is quoted in *Fighting Words*, chapter IV, edited by Donald Ogden Stewart, New York, 1940, pp. 50-53.

[8] 'The Historical Novel', *Fighting Words*, p. 50. Subsequent page references are given in brackets in the text.

[9] *The Historical Novel*, p. 200.

[10] A 'ground' in renaissance music, especially liked in seventeenth-century England, was a more or less unvarying bass figure against which a series of variations were played

[11] Though somewhat differently expressed, there is much shared ground here between Sylvia Townsend Warner's and Lukacs' conception of the problems and value of the historical novel. Thus we can find Lukacs discussing: the 'very complex interaction between his [*sic*: the writers] relation to the present and his relation to history' (p. 199), the necessity for the present to play a part in the authentic historical novel: 'the severance of the present from history creates an historical novel which drops to the level of light entertainment' (p.217) and historical novels in which 'the past is used simply as illustrative material for the problems of the present (p. 347), turning 'the past into a parable of the present' (p.408).

[12] Virago edition, 1987, p.153. All subsequent refernces are to this edition and will be given in the text.

[13] In his article on the 'Historical Novel' in *Encyclopedia of the Novel*, ed. Schelinger, Paul, 1998, Vol. 1

[14] See, for example the discussion in chapters of *The Historical Novel* such as 'Historical Novel and Historical Drama', pp. 196-8.

[15] *Sylvia Townsend Warner – a Biography*, 1989; Minerva edition, 1992, p.150.

[16] *Summer Will Show*: the Historical Novel as Social Criticism', in *Women in History, Literature and the Arts: a Festschrift for Hildegrd Schnuttgen in Honor of her Thirty Years of Outstanding Service at Youngstown State University*, ed. Lorrayne Y. Baird-Lange and Thomas A. Copeland, 1989, p. 263.

[17] 'Dream made Flesh: Sexual Difference and Narratives of Revolution in Sylvia Townsend Warner's *Summer Will Show*' in *Modern Fiction Studies* 1995, 41 (3-4): (pp. 531-62). Also cited by Christina Rauch (see note 21) p.2.

[18] 'Silent Subversions: the Fiction of Sylvia Townsend Warner (1893-1978)' published on the web at http://www.colophon.org/webarch/opcit_onedotzero/winter99/crauch/rauch.htm (read 5.3.03), pp.1-3.

[19] See, for example, p. 1, for discussion of the effect of irony in *After the Death of Don Juan* and p. 3 for Rosemary Sykes' discussion of Sylvia townsend Warner's sense of historiography.

[20] 'Sylvia Townsend Warner: "The Centrifugal Kick" in *Women Writers of the 1930s: Gender, Politics and History* , ed. Maroula Joannou, 1999, p.76

[21] The passage is given in italics in the novel to indicate that it is read from the manuscript of Ingelbrecht's book.

[22] Claire Harman, *Sylvia Townsend Warner – A Biography*, 1989, 1991, p. 149.

[23] J. Lawrence Mitchell in *Writers of the Old School*, ed. Rosemary M. Colt and Janice Rossen, Macmillan, London, 1992, 136

[24] See http://www.colophon.org/webarch/opcit_onedotzero/winter99/crauch/rauch.htm (read 5.3.03)

[25] *Sylvia Townsend Warner - A Biography*, 175.

[26] Virago edition, 1989, p.1. All subsequent page references will be given in the text

[27] ' *Summer Will Show*: the Historical Novel as Social Criticism', in *Women in History, Literature and the Arts: a Festschrift for Hildegrd Schnuttgen in Honor of her Thirty Years of Outstanding Service at Youngstown State University*, ed. Lorrayne Y. Baird-Lange and Thomas A. Copeland, 1989, p. 265.

[28] 'Writing Against the Grain' in *Women's Writing in Exile*,1989.

[29] Penguin translation, Harmondsworth, 1962, p.408 and p. 412.

[30] See his account of the economic structure of his sister's funeral. p.28.

[31] In her Introduction to the Virago edition of the novel, 1989, p. xii.

[32] Introduction to the Virago edition, 1988, pp. v and vii-viii.

[33] As Claire Harman observes in her Introduction to the Virago edition, 1988, p.x

[34] 'A consistently well-imagined chronicle of life in a Fenlands convent', p 216.

[35] Chapter X 'Triste Loysir' has a fuller and technically knowledgable account of how Henry Yellowlees is ravished by this new music with its new ways of counting time and with 'each voice in turn enkindling the others' (p. 204).

[36] Quoted in Claire Harman's introduction to the Virago edition, p. vi

[37] 'Sylvia Townsend Warner: "The Centrifugal Kick" in *Women Writers of the 1930s: Gender, Politics and History* , ed. Maroula Joannou, 1999, p. 82.

CHAPTER 8

The Flint Anchor and the Conventions of Historical Fiction
David Malcolm

The argument of this essay is that Sylvia Townsend Warner's last novel, *The Flint Anchor* (1954), while possessing clear genre markers of historical fiction, substantially deviates from the conventions of the historical novel. This text is dominated, rather, by motifs relating to almost a-historical individual psychology and to very general existential states and experiences. This aspect of the novel can be compared to the balance of the historical and the a-historical in Warner's earlier historical novels, *Summer Will Show* (1936) and *The Corner That Held Them* (1948). These works, in turn, can be seen as part of a tendency to re-examine the nature of the historical novel in mid-twentieth-century British fiction, as illustrated, for example, in the work of Virginia Woolf, T.H. White, Robert Graves, Mary Renault and Alfred Duggan.

Warner's work has often produced an unease among critics; she seems difficult to categorize and place. Highly regarded by many commentators, she misses becoming canonical, in a way that contemporaries like Evelyn Waugh and George Orwell, or even (belatedly) Jean Rhys have become. Eleanor Perényi calls her "that anomaly, the well-known writer who isn't talked about, whose work was too original to be very popular yet who failed to attract a cult audience" (27). Perényi later claims that Warner's anomalous and marginalized position within British fiction is related to the difficulty commentators have in categorizing her. "Feminist, Marxist, historical novelist, social comedian, teller of fairy tales – she was all these, and none of them to a degree that would ultimately define her; and this is her disadvantage. If a convenient pigeonhole could be found for her . . . no doubt we would be in the flood of a Warner revival" (30). Perhaps she is too awkward, too deviant; in a long essay on *Summer Will Show* Terry Castle argues convincingly that Warner defiantly challenges fundamental principles of canonical English and American fiction (Castle 128-147). Be that as it may, Warner's historical novels certainly cock a snook at the conventions of historical fiction. It is worth noting that in *The Flint Anchor*, Ellen, the most oppressed and marginalized of the Barnard children (she has a large strawberry birthmark) is said at one point to be "busy writing a historical novel which of course would never get finished," since, according to Mary, the most socially powerful of the siblings, it is just one of Ellen's "fads" (246). One should also note that Julia Barnard's last night alive begins with her crying out "Murder!" as her husband reads to her from Scott's *Old Mortality* (234). She is responding to his woeful rendition of Scottish dialect, but one might also see her reaction as reflecting the implied author's rejection of the traditional historical novel.

Surprisingly, given its age and widespread currency in Europe and North America, the historical novel has proved difficult for scholars to define, as is pointed out by Joseph W. Turner in his 1979 essay "The Kinds of Historical Fiction" (333-355). However, from the nineteenth century onwards critics have proposed a model of the historical novel that, at base, can be described as reconstructionist. The historical novel pretends to recreate an earlier era for its readers. Thus George Henry Lewes, writing of Scott, notes: "If, for his purposes, he disarranged the order of events a little, no grave historian ever succeeded better in painting the character of the epoch" (34-54); and Brander Matthews in 1901 sees the main task of the historical novel to lie in the recreation of the peculiarities of past times and peoples (3-28). Twentieth-century English (and German) discussions of the historical novel have been greatly influenced by Georg Lukács's *The Historical Novel* (written in German between 1936 and 1937, and first translated into English in 1962). Lukács's first chapter is entitled "The

Classical Form of the Historical Novel" and advances a reconstructionist model of historical fiction.

> The so-called historical novels of the seventeenth century (Scudéry, Calpranède, etc.) are historical only as regards their purely external choice of theme and costume. Not only the psychology of the characters, but the manners depicted are entirely those of the writer's own day. And in the most famous "historical novel" of the eighteenth century, Walpole's *Castle of Otranto* [sic], history is likewise treated as mere costumery: it is only the curiosities and oddities of the *milieu* that matter, not an artistically faithful image of a concrete historical epoch. (15)

Although, with regard to Lukács, one must always recall that his notion of "an unbiased exploration of the real life of the past" (89) is a mid-twentieth-century Marxist/Stalinist one that the contemporary reader might demur at, his principle that a central convention of historical fiction is an act of temporal palingenesis or resuscitation would be uncontroversial to Lewes, Lord Macaulay and Thomas Carlyle (as, for example, in Part IV of his 1838 essay on Scott in the *London and Westminster Review*). Lukács, like Matthews, makes clear that the classic historical novel (which is the only kind Lukács approves of) reconstructs a specific historical world and characters that are constituted by that world so as to make them different from the denizens of later ages. "What is lacking in the so-called historical novel before Sir Walter Scott," he writes, "is precisely the specifically historical, that is, derivation of the individuality of characters from the historical peculiarity of their age" (15). This view of what the classic, nineteenth-century, Scottian historical novel is all about, is endorsed by Morse Peckham. "In Gibbon and other historians," he argues, "there is little or no sense of the pastness of the past, of the otherness of the past, but rather of the sameness. . . . But the otherness of the past, its pastness, the difference in its visual appearance, the strangeness of past modes of interaction – these were precisely what the nineteenth century was interested in. These were precisely the factors which gave the novels of Scott their strength and an appeal still attractive" (279).

Drawing on a range of sources, including Macaulay, Andrew Sanders also points out the centrality of the reconstruction of an alien and idiosyncratic past to the conventions of the classical historical novel that develops in the nineteenth century (4-5), although he also indicates the way that for nineteenth-century writers and readers, historical fiction frequently had a strong relevance to contemporary social, political and moral issues (11). However, critics have also discussed the way in which, in the twentieth century, individual historical novels have distanced themselves from the classic conventions established earlier. In *The English Historical Novel: Walter Scott to Virginia Woolf* (1971), Avrom Fleishman discusses how "Virginia Woolf's two tours de force, *Orlando* (1928) and *Between the Acts* (1941), bring the tradition of the English historical novel to a self-conscious close" (233). He sees Woolf's historical novels as questioning the idea of objectivity that underlies the reconstructionist convention within historical fiction, and argues – with much prescience for his study dates from 1971, more than a decade before novels such as Graham Swift's *Waterland* (1983) and Timothy Mo's *An Insular Possession* (1986) – that what a later commentator calls "historiographical metafiction" will shape the development of the genre (Fleishman 255; Hutcheon 71-91). Reworkings of the nineteenth-century conventions of classic historical fiction also form the subject of Ewald Mengel's more recent study of British historical novels, *Geschichtsbild und Romankonzeption* (1986). He argues that, although many commentators see mid-twentieth-century historical novels not as a continuation or development of the genre, but rather as a degenerate form of it, this period shows challenging and forceful deviations from established conventions, particularly in questioning the inherently progressive aspects of the classic model, but also its reconstructionist ambition (14-15, 22, 27). It is, for the purposes of this essay, striking that neither Fleishman nor Mengel discusses Warner's historical novels in the context of the mid-twentieth century developments of the genre. Yet they play an interesting, if clearly underrated, role in these developments, and demonstrate features comparable to those of writers Fleishman and Mengel do discuss, such as Woolf, T.H. White. William Golding and Mary Renault.[1]

For, by any stretch of the critical imagination, several of Warner's novels are historical novels, or at least clearly show the markers of historical fiction. This is certainly true of *The Flint Anchor*. These markers take three forms: the giving of (predominantly) nineteenth-century dates as temporal signposts; references to historically documented events, institutions and phenomena of other kinds; and allusions to idiosyncratic circumstances of nineteenth-century life. Dates are given at the novel's start in the reproduction of John Barnard's tombstone in Loseby parish church. The reader is told that the protagonist lives from 1790 to 1863 (1). The narrative's progression is punctuated by time markers, such as "It was in the autumn of 1832" (23), "it was the spring of 1835" (35), "It was the first winter of the Hungry Forties" (193), "in 1843" (196), "the Irish Famine" (215), "Basil Cook had died in 1844" (225), "They arrived in Paris on February 20th, and two days later the revolution of 1848 broke out" (228), "They were in the spring of 1852" (233), "by the end of 1853" (246), "It was the summer of 1856" (257), "In 1858" (263), and "In the spring of 1863" (276).

The novel also makes constant references to historical phenomena of various kinds, for example "the Trading Acts" (presumably the Orders in Council of 1807 and later) (8), Napoleon's exile to Elba (12), "the prospect of a Queen of England" (before Victoria's accession in 1837) (83), Chartism in 1848 (229), the great Exhibition of 1851 (233), and the Crimean War (256, 258). In addition, the novel frequently alludes to experiences and circumstances that the implied reader of the novel can be assumed to recognise as specifically belonging to the nineteenth-century past. Such references include that to John Barnard's "quinsy" (8), the "Bleeding, cupping, leeches, strong purges, a lowering diet" prescribed for the Barnards' sick children (30), the Barnards' "newly installed water-closet" (78), Mary's and Thomas's "new-fashioned" habit of calling each other by the first names after marriage (171), Mary's quintessentially 1840s views on the poor and their corruption through charity (195), changing fashions of the 1850s ("the fashion for richer colours, more elaborate ornamentation, and fuller curves") (244), and John Barnard's uneasy response to demonstrations of affection between his daughter and her second husband ("But something, he did not know what, had happened to society, and he moved in a world where his judgements were outdated") (253).

Thus, *The Flint Anchor* clearly demonstrates signs of the genre of historical fiction: there is a clear setting in a sufficiently distant past (more than the arbitrary, but powerful, convention of 'tis sixty years since); the story material is clearly located in relation to greater (and less grand) historical events; and the novel alludes to experiences and attributes of its characters that are idiosyncratic to a specific historical period of around sixty years in the nineteenth century. But despite these signs, *The Flint Anchor* stands apart from the traditional, the "classic" historical novel; its emphasis lies elsewhere in comparison to the inherited conventions of the genre (in mid-century and at its time of writing). This is apparent in two (related) aspects of the text – its focus on virtually a-historical psychological states, and on very general existential states and experiences. These shift the novel in the direction of a variant of the social psychological novel (or novel of manners).

Critics have often shown themselves aware of the complex relation of Warner's historical fictions to their ostensible genre. Wendy Mulford insists on the historicity of the relationships portrayed in *Summer Will Show* (104), but other commentators show a hesitancy about this aspect of her work. For example, W.J. Strachan writes of *The Corner That Held Them* that it "hardly follows the lines of a traditional historical narrative" (41-42). Manning notes that Warner "views her fourteenth-century nuns through twentieth-century eyes" (744), and Anthony West praises *The Flint Anchor* because it "escapes the usual *longueurs* of the novel that abandons the present for the past by being . . . psychologically profound about family relationships" (175). He also describes it as "almost imperceptibly, a historical novel" (175). Castle refers to "the framing pretence of historicity" in *Summer Will Show* (qtd. in "Warner" 346). It is notable that Gay

Wachman's analysis of *The Flint Anchor* focuses on the consequences of what she calls "Victorian hypocrisy" (181) (in fact, Barnard is really a Georgian, a man of the Regency, not a Victorian), rather than the particular configuration of that hypocrisy (73, 181). In her biography of Warner, Claire Harman, while declaring that "the evocation of early nineteenth-century Norfolk [is] deft and thoroughly convincing" (255), points out with reference to *The Corner That Held Them* that it is "not a historical novel, but a piece of highly artificial 'realism'" (216). (One does not have to agree with Harman's terminology to suggest that her unease about what to call Warner's historical fictions is well founded, just as one does not have to agree with Wachman's diagnosis of Barnard as a hypocrite.) However, despite the interest of critics in the topic, the ways in which Warner reworks historical fiction, especially in *The Flint Anchor*, remain to be explored.

The focus in *The Flint Anchor* on psychological experiences that are only historically specific in quite minor ways is most apparent in its treatment of the protagonist, John Barnard. From the very start of the novel, his psychology belongs not to the early nineteenth century alone, but is presented in a-historical terms. Thus, when he learns that he has to take on the family business, his sentiments are presented as follows: "From feeling that an intolerable burden had been cast upon him, John Barnard presently came to feel that he had been called in the nick of time" (4). The past participle "called," with its evangelical Protestant connotations, is here the only term that might place Barnard's attitude in a specific historical context, but the text does not so locate it, and the connotations have at least a four-hundred-year validity. The de-historicizing of Barnard's psychological make-up is even more marked as the novel proceeds. For example, his feelings about his daughter Mary are presented in this way. "But a new ingredient had been thrown into his ferment of anxiety, conscience, and idealism," the reader is told. "The new ingredient was love, passionate, romantic love, and its object was his third daughter, Mary" (17). One should note here the abstract lexis ("anxiety, conscience, and idealism"). Further, even the potentially period term "romantic" is de-historicized by being spelt in lower case, and because, as the reader learns in the course of the novel, Barnard's devotion to his daughter is a devoted, emotionally blind one, and is "romantic" in a loose modern sense of the word, rather than in a sense specific to early nineteenth-century European culture. The non-period configuration of Barnard's psychology is evident throughout the novel. Thus, with regard to Mary again, the reader learns "It was as if he had received a licence with her, an unconditional permit to love one child, free of tax or charges against deterioration" (20). Barnard's reflections on Mary's possible death on the following page (21) are also relevant here, as are his experience of watching Mary walking in the garden on an autumn morning (24), his attitude towards his elder daughter Euphemia (33), and his sudden realization that his marriage has gone stale ("Twenty-four years ago, he had Julia, and how and when he had lost her he did not know" [133]).

When Barnard, towards the novel's end, comes to formulate his failings and errors, and deep sense of loss, he does so still in terms that are almost entirely a-historical (apart again from the slight evangelical Protestant flavour of the opening sentence). He is addressing his youngest son.

> Give not your heart to idols! That is what I did, Wilberforce – your sister Mary. I know it at last. I loved her inordinately. Inordinately, Wilberforce. Everything has gone wrong because of that. Everything that came between me and her was an impediment. I trod it down or thrust it away. All of you, and your mother too – I have sacrificed everything to an inordinate love. You might say that I deluded myself, but I deluded myself deliberately. I plotted with myself to remain deluded. (273)

One can note the same in Barnard's long interior monologue in the Loseby churchyard, largely given in free indirect speech, in which he reflects on passing time and wasted chances (278-279). His experience on his deathbed is similarly a-historical – "It was horrible. Only her [Mary's] tears had any truth in them, being paid to death. Everything else was completely false. He tried to move his hand away. . . . He shut his eyes and tried to compose himself, but after a few minutes he began to hiccough. He covered his face with his hands to veil his agony" (281-281). This is not specifically a death in 1863, but a generally human one.

Warner's strategy in *The Flint Anchor* of focussing on a-historical psychological experience is also apparent in the presentation of other characters in the novel. Barnard's dying son Julius asks for a chestnut and when his father brings him several strokes them as they lie on his bed, and suddenly notes that his father's hair is grey (32). Like his father's death later in the novel, this scene transcends any particular period. Marmaduke Debenham's visit brings pleasure to Julia Barnard. "After so many years of existing on the confused remnants of the young woman who had married John Barnard, Julia, in a couple of minutes, achieved a glorious climacteric, and was an old woman enjoying herself" (37). She later formulates her character in a way that transcends the particular – "I drink. I am a drunkard. I have been a drunkard for the last twenty years" (213). Even though aspects of Euphemia's situation in the novel are determined by patriarchal authority and whim, this is not just a feature of early nineteenth-century British life alone, nor is it presented as such (88-89), while her despairing reflections on her desire to escape are seen in the broadest of terms. "Her scheming suddenly seemed to her no more than a nuisance, a scroll-work on which she had wasted time and debased herself. Why go to Herrnhut rather than to the Bay of Naples, when all one had to do was to wait a little, and then die?" (222). The movements of Thomas's mind are similarly presented. For example, there is nothing in his thoughts as he walks round Loseby to fix them in the mid-1830s.

> Turning again in his walking to and fro, he saw that the western sky was drained of its sunset, only a rusty tint remaining on the clouds that had burned so long and so brilliantly. Lighted windows peered out, and the smell of the town came greasily puffing towards him. Six months ago he had not even heard of Loseby. Now it was the place where he must be his father's son. (57)

Nor is there any historical specificity in his fears of remaining in Anchor House after the scandal of his being accused of homosexuality (179), and neither is there any in his sense that he has lost a battle for his wife with her father (180). The same can be argued about Daniel and John Barnard's feelings about each other when they meet in London in the late 1840s.

> John Barnard felt a childish impulse to confide in his brother. Daniel's ungloved hand, resting on the parapet, caught his eye, and he thought how it and his own had been shaped in the same womb. Staring into the fog, Daniel said, "Robina's got cancer." The words scattered the illusion of intimacy. The nursery brothers were two ageing men, each meshed in his own net of calamity. (227)

Wilberforce's musings on his relationship with his father (259-260) are similarly a-historical, reflections on the complexities of family relationships that are not tied to the particular time of the novel's setting. *The Flint Anchor* is a novel interested in psychological states, but those psychological states are not made specific to the 1830s or the 1840s.

Two other features of the novel reinforce one's sense of its psychological and a-historical focus. These are the narrational technique of shifting points of view, and the relatively modern language which narrators and characters use. *The Flint Anchor* combines the point of view of an omniscient third-person narrator with that of individual characters. John Barnard's point of view is the one given most often, but the narrator switches to that of other characters with considerable frequency, sometimes moving from that of one character to another in close order. A good example of this technique is Euphemia's and Marmaduke's first meeting in 1835. The encounter is presented through Euphemia's thoughts – it is preceded by her reflections on her unmarried state and her sense of what her physical circumstances are just before his visit. When Marmaduke is introduced, the narrator gives her thought almost directly: "Her first impression was Whippersnapper" (35). (The lack of article before "Whipper-snapper" suggests an unmediated rendition of Euphemia's response.) A few lines later, the narrator supplies Marmaduke's impression through free indirect speech: "So this was the girl who had written those letters." Two paragraphs of his thoughts and memories follow, and then after a few lines of dialogue, the narration moves to Euphemia's point of view, radically shifting into free direct speech (that is, a character's thoughts, given directly, but not enclosed within quotation marks): "Why have I no presence of mind? Why don't I get him out of the house while I can? Why shouldn't Mamma see him?" (36). Many other examples could be generated from the text, and the technique as a whole emphasizes the fundamentally psychological orientation of the novel.

The linguistic configuration of *The Flint Anchor* also confirms the a-historical nature of the psychological experiences presented there. In a review of *The Corner That Held Them* Olivia Manning notes that Warner makes no "attempt . . . to fit out her nuns with archaic language and thoughts" (744). Neither narrator nor characters in *The Flint Anchor* use anything that could be clearly classed as archaic, nineteenth-century English. For example, after Joseph Barnard has abandoned Cambridge and run off to the West Indies, a distressed John Barnard returns home.

> Euphemia was the first person he met with on his return. The kettle-holder came into his mind, and he began to question her. He did not expect to learn much by this, but it was his duty to follow every clue. Euphemia, as usual, was sullen and reserved, and he tripped her almost at once.
> "I gave it to him because I thought it might be useful."
> "Then you must have known what was in his mind. Where would a kettle-holder be useful?"
> "Almost anywhere, I suppose, if one wanted to make tea."
> "Euphemia, do not prevaricate. You cannot put me off so easily. Where is your brother?"
> "I don't know."
> "You only injure him by this concealment. Euphemia, my dear child, I know you love your brother. Surely you wish to help him, to rescue him from misery, from destitution or profligacy?"
> In a considering tone of voice she said, "Yes."
> "Then tell me where you think he is."
> "I do not know."

He sent her away at last, and sat on in despair. (26)

Here only the sentence "Euphemia, do not prevaricate" and the phrase "to rescue him from misery, from destitution or profligacy" locate the characters in the early nineteenth century. Predominantly narration and direct speech are conducted in at most a rather formal, and mostly quite neutral, modern English. Once again, the novel's action is partly de-historicized.

Further, *The Flint Anchor* is not really a novel about historically specific states and experiences, but about almost universal existential apprehensions, particularly that of transience.[2] Characters' emotions and observations are put in broad, at times abstract, contexts. John Barnard develops a "trammelled conscience" when young (5); like the nuns her mother sees in Paris, Euphemia makes "her renunciation" (117); Barnard is assaulted by "the Black Dog" of depression (143); Julia sees her own life, and that of her daughter, clearly in the context of the grinding rigours of women's lives in general ("how long it takes to live, if one is a woman, thought Julia") (189); "Nothing could be put right," Barnard dismally concludes of life in general when thinking about Thomas (226); once Barnard falls out of love with his daughter he reflects that "Love had gone, and as the flames ran up the chimney he realised that when love goes, fear goes with it" (269). Narrational technique plays a role here, for the narrator herself constantly generalizes the characters' situations and experiences. For example, of Sophie Kettle the narrator remarks that she is "a woman and the more socially sensitive animal" (114). "There is a give-and-take in all traffic between deluder and deluded," she notes of Mutty and Mrs Kettle (116), and later of Mary's response to Thomas's disgrace: "Women conduct life as they conduct their needlework" (191). "Peter was happy; and a happy man can never be much in the wrong," the reader is informed in relation to Mary's second husband (254), and during Barnard's interior monologue in the churchyard at the novel's end, the narrator slips in her own observation that "the domestic voice of the clock is always admonishing one of the nature of time, but one listens to it thinking of hours and appointments" (279).

This last quotation is *à propos*, for one of the ways in which the *The Flint Anchor* indicates its a-historicity is through recurrent motifs of transience, of transience as a general existential state, and not one particularly connected to the specificities of life in eastern England between 1790 and 1863. Such motifs occur throughout the text. Impermanence haunts the novel (as it does *Summer Will Show* and *The Corner That Held Them*). Early in the text, Julia opines to herself that "Children die, teeth decay. Only weight accumulates and faithfully remains" (14). John Barnard reflects on Mary's possible death when "the worms would devour her flesh" (21), and his vision of her in the autumn garden is a classic and baroque one of the mutability of beauty and youth (24). The chestnuts he lays out for his dying son, and the son's suddenly calling out "Papa! Your hair is grey" (32) are also part of this pattern of motifs, as are Mary's feelings after being kissed by Thomas (124-125). The graveyard at Herrnhut is a large-scale *memento mori* (137), and so is the one in which Barnard spends his latter years, a graveyard not simply full of the graves of others, but also of his own wife and children (266-267). "Why go to Herrnhut rather than to the bay of Naples, when all one had to do was to wait a little and then die?" Euphemia asks herself (222). Wilberforce walks through his mother's dressing room after her death, and, all the while thinking of Latin quotes that emphasize transience, notes the shabby relics of the past that it contains (240-241), relics that are later gathered by Ellen in the garret in Anchor House where she and her father take refuge from the present (261-263). "Nothing could give him back his heart which an error of love had eaten out as a worm eats the hazel kernel," Barnard reflects towards the end of his life (277). His late interior monologue in Loseby churchyard is similarly full of regret for missed and irrecoverable chances, a regret expressed through traditional motifs of impermanency, the gravestone, the clock, and the waves of the sea (278-279).

Part of this sequence of motifs (and a source of much poignancy in the novel) are characters' brief moments of joy, endlessly cherished and regretted.

Julia recalls "those airy few weeks in the lodgings near Portsmouth" before her marriage (14). For Thomas, the brief fishing expedition on the *Mary Lucinda* (58-61) is a central instant of happiness in an otherwise failed life, one that distinguishes him, he feels, and one to which he returns in memory (69, 151). For a brief time, too, he is happy in Snipe Cottage with Mary – and she is too (148). He recalls that transient joy in his final letter to her (202). Even in Barnard's misguided, disappointed and arid life, there are points of fleeting transcendence – notably, when he looks after the sick Thomas ("he presently began to enjoy himself") (168), and on a trip to Brighton with his ageing brother ("It gave him a sense of exhilaration and release") (227). *The Flint Anchor* is not only full of motifs of *memento mori*, but also of *carpe diem*.

Thus, *The Flint Anchor*, like much of Warner's work, occupies a borderland, in this case on the margins of the historical novel traditionally understood. While demonstrating some of the accepted conventions of the genre (dating, a relation to documented events, a historical specificity), it nevertheless constantly verges off in the direction of a strongly psychologically oriented variant of the novel of manners, and, indeed, at times becomes markedly de-historicized in its deployment of universal motifs of transience.

Both *Summer Will Show* and *The Corner That Held Them* possess some similar features. The action of the former is certainly embedded in historical events (the revolutionary events of 1848 in Paris, among others), and the reader is constantly aware of the historical specificity of Sophia's situation and experience. However, the text also de-historicizes her by a focus on almost a-historical psychological states (loss, frustration, jealousy, pleasure), and by Warner's resolute avoidance of archaic nineteenth-century language ("Hullo, Sophia! How long have you been in Paris?" says Frederick to her on meeting her at Minna Lemuel's soirée [367]). One can – *mutatis mutandis* – say the same of *The Corner That Held Them*. Pernelle's feelings for Jackie (645), Prioress Alicia's sense of disappointment after the completion of the spire (670), or Sir Ralph's afternoon reading in Brocton (694-695), for example, are not presented as historically specific, but rather as a-historical mental and emotional conditions, and, along with the un-medieval language of the text, wrench the novel out of its largely fourteenth-century setting.

As Mengel indicates in *Geschichtsbild und Romankonzeption*, the mid-twentieth-century historical novel in Britain develops in a complex and multi-vocal fashion. The traditional historical novel is alive and well, as in, for example, Robert Graves's Claudius novels (*I, Claudius* and *Claudius the God* [both 1934]), or in Alfred Duggan's novels, such as *Knight with Armour* (1950). The traditional historical romance sub-genre, which has always co-existed, sometimes inextricably, with the historical novel, is similarly robust – in, for example, Georgette Heyer's more than forty fictions, published between 1921 and 1975.[3] There is also an innovative engagement with historical fiction in the work of T.H. White, especially *The Once and Future King* tetralogy of novels (1938-1958) (which Mengel discusses at length [259-262]), and in Virginia Woolf's *Orlando* (1928) and *Between the Acts* (1941) (both of which Fleishman discusses [233-255]), but also in William Golding's radically inventive pre-historical novel *The Inheritors* (1955). In addition, Mary Renault's historical novels (published between 1955 and 1981) – for example, *Fire from Heaven* (1969), a strongly psychologized portrait of Alexander the Great – show a complex engagement with the conventions of the genre. This re-writing of the genre is clearly continued in the work of Paul Scott and J.G. Farrell. Although critics note that the complex historical fictions of the 1980s and 1990s by Salman Rushdie, Graham Swift, Timothy Mo and Kazuo Ishiguro, for example, do not spring from nowhere, a detailed examination of the development of the historical novel in mid-twentieth-century Britain, a development in which Warner surely plays a key role, might be very illuminating.[4]

English Institute of the University of Gdansk

Works Cited

Castle, Terry. "Sylvia Townsend Warner and the Counterplot of Lesbian Fiction." *Sexual Sameness: Textual Differences in Lesbian and Gay Writing*. Ed. Joseph Bristow. London: Routledge, 1992: 128-147.

Fleishman, Avrom. *The English Historical Novel: Walter Scott to Virginia Woolf*. Baltimore and London: The John Hopkins P, 1971.

Harman, Claire. *Sylvia Townsend Warner: A Biography*. London: Chatto and Windus, 1989.

Hutcheon, Linda. "Historiographic Metafiction." *Metafiction*. Ed. Mark Currie. London and New York: Longman, 1995.

Lukács, Georg. *The Historical Novel*. 1962. Trans. Hannah and Stanley Middleton. Harmondsworth: Penguin, 1976.

Lewes, George Henry. Review essay. *The Westminster Review* 45.1 (March1846): 34-54.

Matthews, Brander. "The Historical Novel." *The Historical Novel and Other Essays*. New York: Charles Scribner Sons, 1901: 3-28.

Manning, Olivia. Rev. of *The Corner That Held Them* by Sylvia Townsend Warner. *The Spectator* 3 Dec. 1948: 744.

Mengel, Ewald. *Geschichtsbild und Romankonzeption: Drei Typen des Geschichtsverstehens im Reflex der Form des englischen historischen Romans*. Anglistische Forschungen 190. Heidelberg: Carl Winter-Universitätsverlag, 1986.

Mulford, Wendy. *This Narrow Place: Sylvia Townsend Warner and Valentine Ackland: Life, Letters and Politics, 1930-1951*. Kitchener, Canada: Pandora Press, 1988.

Peckham, Morse. "Afterword: Reflections on Historical Modes in the Nineteenth Century." *Victorian Poetry*. Ed. Malcolm Bradbury and David Palmer. Stratford-Upon-Avon Studies 15. London: Arnold, 1972: 277-300.

Perényi, Eleanor. "The Good Witch of the West." *New York Review of Books* 32 (18 July 1985): 27-30.

161

Sanders, Andrew. *The Victorian Historical Novel 1840-1880*. London and Basingstoke: Macmillan, 1978.

Strachan, W.J. "Sylvia Townsend Warner: A Memoir." *London Magazine* 19.8 (Nov. 1979): 41-50.

Turner, Joseph W. "The Kinds of Historical Fiction: An Essay in Definition and Methodology." *Genre* 12.3 (Fall 1979): 333-355.

Wachman, Gay. *Lesbian Empire: Radical Crosswriting in the Twenties*. New Brunswick, NJ, and London: Rutgers UP, 2001.

Warner, Sylvia Townsend. *Summer Will Show*. 1936. *Four in Hand: A Quartet of Novels – Sylvia Townsend Warner*. Intr. William Maxwell. New York: W.W. Norton, 1986.

———. *The Corner That Held Them*. 1948. *Four in Hand: A Quartet of NovelsSylvia Townsend Warner*. Intr. William Maxwell. New York: W.W.Norton, 1986.

———. *The Flint Anchor*. 1954. London: Virago, 1997.

"Warner, Sylvia Townsend." *Twentieth-Century Literary Criticism*. Vol. 131. Detroit, New York, San Diego etc.: Thomson/Gale, 2003.

West, Anthony. Rev. of *The Flint Anchor* by Sylvia Townsend Warner. *The New Yorker* 9 October 1954: 175.

Notes

[1] For excellent discussions of "historiographical metafiction," see: Asgar Nünning, "Grenzüberschreitungen: Neue Tendenzen im historischen Roman" in Annegret Maack and Rüdiger Imhof, eds., *Radikalität und Ermäßigung: Der englische Roman seit 1960* (Darmstadt: Wissenschaftliche Buchgesellschaft, 1993): 54-73; Frederick M. Holmes, *The Historical Imagination: Postmodernism and the Treatment of the Past in Contemporary British Fiction* (Victoria, Canada: University of Victoria, 1973); and Andrzej Gąsiorek, *Post-War British Fiction: Realism and After* (London and New York: Arnold, 1995).

[2] Scott is, *pace* Lukács, ambiguous on the matter of historical specificity as opposed to universality. In chapter 1 of *Waverley*, the narrator/implied author tells the reader that his focus is on "those passions common to men in all stages of society. . . . Upon these passions it is no doubt true that the state of manners and laws casts a necessary colouring; but the bearings, to use the

language of heraldry, remain the same, though the tincture may be not only different, but opposed in strong contradistinction." This seems to be having things both ways.

[3] For a recent and most illuminating study of Heyer's fiction see: Lisa Fletcher, "Mere Costumery" in Jesús López-Peláez Casellas, David Malcolm and Pilar Sánchez Calle, eds., *Masquerades: Disguise in Literature in English from the Middle Ages to the Present* (Gdańsk: Gdańsk UP, 2004): 196-212. Fletcher's observation of a shift from adventure-story action to love-story materials in the genre (or sub-genre) parallels my discussion of the psychologizing and de-historicizing of historical fiction in Warner's work.

[4] In this respect, see: Bernard Bergonzi, "Fictions of History" in Malcolm Bradbury and David Palmer, eds., *The Contemporary English Novel* (London: Arnold, 1979): 43-65; and Bradbury, *The Modern British Novel* (Harmondsworth: Penguin, 1994): 404. For a discussion of this issue, see: David Malcolm, *That Impossible Thing: The British Novel 1978-1992* (Gdańsk: Gdańsk UP, 2000): 13-18.

INDEX

Ackland, Valentine, i, iv, v, 16, 19, 22, 25, 29-43, 56, 61, 63
Anzaldùa, G., 90, 95
Baldwin, S., 62, 67,79, 80
Basile, G., 52, 53
Beer, G., ii, 126, 141
Bakhtin, M.M., 3, 4, 7, 10, 75, 98
Beckford, W., 53
Brothers, B., 125, 132, 154
Burns, R., 72
Butterfield, H., 104, 106
Carlyle, T., 147
Carpenter, E., 85, 86
Carter, A., ii, 54
Castle, T., 16-18, 125, 160
Clare, J., 62, 68-9, 72-3
Cobbett, W., 72
Cunard, N., iv
Derrida, J., 14-5, 98
Duggan, A., 145, 159
Dunsanay, Lord, 56
Eddison, E.R., 56
Empson, W., 65-6, 71, 77
Engels, F., 62
Farrell, J.G., 159
Fleishman, A., 148-9, 159
Foster, T., 125
Fox, R. 118
Garnett, D., 8, 12, 17-26, 55, 76
Garnett, R., 12
Galland, A., 53
Gibbons, S., 67-8, 70
Gibbs, P., 149, 159
Golding, R., 159

Graves, R., 159
Hall, R., 145
Hallett, 12
Hammond, J.L. & B., 62, 72
Harman, C., 17, 25, 83, 125, 136, 151
Henderson, P., 118
Horowitz, L., 13-14
Hutcheon, L., 148
Hogg, J., 49
Ishiguro, K., 159
Johnson, S., 12-4, 25, 53
Keating, A., 98-9
Kirk, R., 49
Knoll, B., 92
Kristeva, J., 99-100
Lang, A., 49, 56
Le Guin, U., 64
Lewes, G.H., 146-7
Lukacs, G., 118, 122, 124, 128, 132, 139
Marie de France, 46-7, 50-53
Marsh, J. 62
Marx, K., 122, 123, 134
Macaulay, Lord, 147-8
Matthews, B., 146
Maxwell, R., 103, 112, 124
Maxwell, W., 17, 55, 118, 161
McClintock, A., 99
Mengel, E., 148, 159
Mo, T., 148
Montefiore, J., 20, 106-7
Morris, W., 56, 62, 72
Morrison, T., 97, 99
Mulford, W., 3, 150, 160

Murat, Comtesse de, 53, 56
Orwell, G., 145
Paulin, T., 17
Pearce, L., 16
Peckham, M., 147, 160
Percy, T., 48
Perrault, C., 53
Postgate, R.W., 104-5
Powys, T.F., 67-8, 70-1
Pratt, M.L., 100
Priestley, J.B., 63
Rattenbury, A., iv, v
Rauch, C., 125, 130
Redford, B., 13
Renault, M., 145, 149, 159
Ribeiro, A., 14
Rickword, C.H., 107
Rigby, N., 86-7, 94-95
Robertson-Scott, J.W., 63-65, 72, 74
Rhys, J., 145
Scott, W., 47-54, 56
Stevenson, R., 93
Shloss, C., 98
Swift, G., 13
Thatcher, M., 58
Thomas, E., 30-31, 34-35, 68, 72, 122-123, 125
Tomlin, S., 18
Trevelyan, G.M., 106
Turner, J.W., 146
Virgil, 64, 66, 73, 74
- *Eclogues,* 64, 66
- *Georgics,* 64, 73
Volosinov, V., 15
Voltaire, 53, 85, 95
Wachman, G., 85, 151
Warner, G. T., 105, 108, 112
Warner, Sylvia Townsend,
Works by:
- *After the Death of Don Juan,* iii, 4, 6, 9, 117, 124, 130-3, 135-6, 140
- 'The Blameless Triangle', 54-5
- 'But at the Stroke of Midnight', 38
- *The Cat's Cradle Book,* 33

- *The Corner That Held Them,* iii, 4, 7, 9, 40, 108-9, 117-8, 135-6, 140-1, 145, 150-1, 155, 157-8
- *The Espalier,* 18, 61, 67
- *I'll Stand by You,* 2
- *The Listening Woman,* 33, 39
- *Kingdoms of Elfin,* 46-8, 51-7
- *Lost Summer,* 39
- 'A Love Match', 106
- *Lolly Willowes,* ii, 2, 4, 18, 38, 41, 61, 68, 73, 76, 79, 80, 107-8
- *Mr Fortune's Magott,* ii, 4, 5, 9, 61, 79, 107
- 'The Mortal Milk', 45
- 'My Shirt is in Mexico', 36
- 'The Music at Long Verney', 38
- 'Five Black Swans', 30-31, 34, 49
- *The Flint Anchor,* iii, v, 1, 8, 9, 41, 145-6, 149-51, 153-58
- 'Foxcastle', 49-50
- 'The Occupation', 48, 50
- 'The One and the Other', 49
- *Opus 7, 61, 65, 67, 69, 71, 72*
- *The Portrait of a Tortoise,* 57-59
- *The Salutation,* 61, 71, 83
- 'A Scent of Roses', 31
- 'The Search for an Ancestress', 54-55
- *Summer Will Show,* ii, iii, 4, 5, 9, 37, 41, 58, 103, 105, 107, 117, 124-6, 129, 130, 132, 135, 136, 140, 141, 145-6, 150, 157-8
- *T. H. White: A Biography,* 11, 21
- *Time Importuned,* 61
- *The True Heart,* ii, 61, 66, 68, 70, 73, 74-5, 78-80
- 'The Way by Which I Have Come', 2
- 'Two Children', 32
- 'Visitors to a Castle', 52
- *Whether a Dove or a Seagull,* 1
Webb, M., 62-3, 67, 70-1
White, E.W., 16
White, G., 57-8
White, T.H., 2, 20-2, 25
Wilde, O., 56

Winterson, J., ii
Woolf, V., 14
Zipes, J., 56